Dedication for the revised edition

To our youngest grandchildren, Davina Teresa Sienkiewicz and Severn Clare Sienkiewicz, this small book is dedicated with utmost joy, gratitude, and abiding love.

Born to our sons and their wonderful wives, Davina and Severn are cousins. Like legendary Snow White and Rose Red, Davina is a blue-eyed blonde, Severn a brown-eyed brunette; each so clever and affectionate, each so bursting with personality. They dance like sunbeams in my soul as I dream of our next visit — and of the years when we can use this book together!

January– 2005

Accept this token from a friend
Whose love for you will never end.
—— old verse

For _____

From _____

Date _____

Place _____

Elly Sienkiewicz
Appliqué
Paper Greetings

A Quilt Approach to Scrapbooking

American Quilter's Society
P. O. Box 3290 • Paducah, KY 42002-3290
www.AmericanQuilter.com

Located in Paducah, Kentucky, the American Quilter's Society (AQS), is dedicated to promoting the accomplishments of today's quilters. Through its publications and events, AQS strives to honor today's quiltmakers and their work — and inspire future creativity and innovation in quiltmaking.

EXECUTIVE EDITOR: JANE R. MCCAULEY
EDITOR: HELEN SQUIRE
BOOK DESIGN: ELAINE WILSON
ILLUSTRATIONS: ELAINE WILSON
COVER DESIGN: TERRY WILLIAMS
PHOTOGRAPHY: CHARLES R. LYNCH, UNLESS OTHERWISE NOTED

Library of Congress Cataloging-in-Publication Data

Sienkiewicz, Elly.
        Appliqué paper greetings / Elly Sienkiewicz.
             p.   cm.
        ISBN 0-89145-898-0 hardcover
        ISBN 1-57432-869-7 paperback
        1. Greeting cards. 2. Paper work. 3. Appliqué. 4. Fusible
material in sewing.   I. Title.
        TT872.S54   1997
        745.594'1--dc21   97-26078
                                                               CIP

Additional copies of this book may be ordered from the American Quilter's Society, PO Box 3290, Paducah, KY 42002-3290; 800-626-5420 (orders only please); or online at www.Americanquilter.com. For all other inquiries, call 270-898-7903.

Appliqué Paper Greetings is dedicated to teachers, especially those whose sense of wonder so long ago slipped into my soul: to my Nana who had me visit with her flowers; to my father whose research into physics was a religious pursuit; and to my mother who loved beauty and taught my Sunday School class how miracles abound through snowflakes and garden snails. To Mrs. Casey who taught us second graders how to identify this country's cattle and birds so that I never can see these creatures without trying to name them; to Miss Bantle who taught me in third grade that an unrelated adult can also be a friend. She visited with me on the playground and encouraged me to make a tabletop model of a Neanderthal dwelling site. She began my fascination with ancient things from fossils, to the dawn of civilizations, to old Baltimore album quilts. My path to the present has been privileged with other excellent teachers as well.

Work of the hands brings me peace. When we are peaceful, we are happy. And when we are happy, we comfort and cheer those around us. To my colleagues who this day teach both the heart and the hand, thank you for making our world happier. May you enjoy this book and journey here with kindred spirits — stitchers, cutters, quilters, card makers and scrapbookers!

Happy New Year!

Karey, Your optimism will be
rewarded (however it all turns out.)
Fondly, Elly S

Acknowledgments

With admiration and gratitude to guest designers Betty Alderman and Nancy Hearndon who made cards especially for this book and to my creative friends whose cards offer inspiration: Carol Elliot, Faye Labanaris, Doris Gilbert, Lois Charles, Bonnie Campbell, Debbie Niel, Kathie Campbell, Julie Russell, Kathy Galos, Irene Keating, Kathleen Brassfield, and the proprietresses of the Quilting Barn in Harbor Springs, Michigan. Thank you for your generous sharing.

To my friends and family, Donald and Katja, Alex and Holly, and Katya, and Stan — thank you for the joys shared and the sorrows assuaged.

Appliqué Paper Greetings focuses on a familiar bird of happiness — the greeting card we make and send. Such smiles this humble creature inspires! For the thoughtful remembrances to which this book gives wing, for the smiles it lights up, thank you folks, one and all, from the bottom of my heart!

My heartfelt thanks to those who worked to make this new edition possible:
To my publisher, Meredith Schroeder and her talented staff at AQS for bringing this enhanced book to print… .

To my editor, Helen Squire, whose marketing enthusiasm and savvy recognized *Appliqué Paper Greetings* as perfect for the burgeoning scrapbooking field. She proposed to make this connection clear in a revised edition… and succeeded. Perhaps only Helen could so persuade a busy author that "We'll make it so easy for you – it won't take much of your time!"… and make her words come true!

To Marjorie Russell, editor of the *American Quilter* magazine, who commissioned and beautifully presented my article drawing the connection between Album Quilts and Scrapbooking (*American Quilter,* Spring 2005). That assignment got this revision underway.

Two talented, generous needle artists made the scrapbook pages for the article and for this book. Long-time colleagues and friends, I can never thank Betty and Earlina enough. Betty is of Betty Alderman Designs, author of *Favorite Appliqué & Embroidery Quilts* and *Favorite Redwork Designs*. Earlina Scott designs and teaches appliqué. She is on the staff of the Elly Sienkiewicz Appliqué Academy, Inc.

Left. *Photo credit: Elly Sienkiewicz.*

Contents

Author's Preface

In a card shop, people browse. They spend a while looking for the right card. The right card's cover attracts them, and what's inside confirms its appeal. We're each looking for a greeting design and message that expresses the wish we want to send. Sometimes we're not quite sure what we want to say. Some feelings are hard to put into words. But we know the suitable card when we see it. Just by sending the card we can convey remembrance and caring.

All my life I've been sent a birthday card or two. I look forward to it. There are people I can count on not to let me down. They are dear to me. I remember as a child my grandmother, Nana, always sent a card. Often it had a $10 bill in it. I loved her cards, I loved the ritual of writing her a thank-you note in return. Nana chose elegant note cards, an affordable echo of her plusher times. She must have dabbed them with perfume. They smelled good, like her home, like her. She'd say, "You'll remember this smell and think of me after I'm gone." I still ask for her perfume, Maillot's Crêpe de Chine, hoping to purchase it somewhere. I still have her outdated box of modish gloves and her note cards, saved (too pretty to use) from her things when she died decades ago. Easily stored, cards have since Victorian times often been kept for posterity. This fact lends our own card making a promise of earthly immortality.

Uncle Jack, my step-grandfather, was Nana's third and last husband. He outlived her by many years. Reserved and frugal, he came as a widower to live with my parents during my university years. I remember the annual Valentine he sent to me at my dorm, where every afternoon the metal mail box wall held anticipation or disappointment. His card was always the small, flat, shaped kind that elementary schoolchildren hand out in quantity. Maybe he bought a box to carry on Nana's card tradition. Maybe it was his somewhat shy way of staying in touch with friends and family. My boyfriend for the bulk of my college years was a dud on Valentine's and other sentimental occasions. But I always had at least one card in my school mailbox — Uncle Jack's small Valentine. It was never signed (and so are traditions made) but always appreciated. Thinking of him and times gone by brought a smile to my face year after year then and still does today.

Without words a greeting card says I'm thinking of you. Happy birthday expresses the universal wish, "I hope you have a happy birthday. Today we all celebrate you. I hope the coming year goes well for you and brings you health and happiness." Greeting cards are connectors, they convey our feelings for each other. "I'm happy for you, sad for you, excited for you, thinking of you on this special occasion. I care for you, I miss you, I need you, I support you, I appreciate you, I want to cheer you up, I want to congratulate you, I want to send my greetings. I want to stay in touch. You are important to me. I count you in my blessings. I think of you during this holiday season when I want to express my fondness and appreciation for my friends, my love for family, my hopes for health, peace, and happiness, especially for you who mean so much to me."

I don't remember card shops in my youth. There must have been some, but surely there are more now. They have become as popular as bookstores. The occasions for sending cards have multiplied. Just today, next to the birthday cards, I saw new categories on the drugstore rack: cope, congratulations, support, friendship, consolation, spirit, and encouragement. This market place trend seems to reflect the growing appreciation we have for each other as we recognize our need for and indebtedness to community. In this time and country where we have so much material wealth, we've come to place a high value on the things that money can't buy. We appreciate the simple pleasure of creating and giving a handmade token of affection. We appreciate those near and dear who give us warmth and offer comfort in a large and fast-paced world. While technology speeds up our lives, we hunger for those old-fashioned activities that slow us down enough to experience what we value in life. Card making and card giving are a satisfying response to our yearnings to stop and smell the flowers and reach out and touch someone. Popularly, we are advised to care for our souls, to savor the present, live in the moment, and rejoice in being alive. Card making does just that: The process evokes the beauty of the here and now.

Greetings are cultural customs. A bow in Japan, a handshake in the United States, a "hello, how are you today" in the grocery store, are signals of goodwill. To withhold them shows either hostility or poor form. No less ritualized are sympathy cards, birthday greetings, and thank-you notes. The ritual changes from country to country and from era to era. Today, more Americans live longer, eat better, read more, and have more health care, more creature comforts, and more enabling technology than at any time or in any place before. The downside of things makes news and urges improvement. But the quiet, often unspoken needs are eternal ones: for community, for friendship, to feel needed, and to have caring human attachments. What seems freshly contemporary is the trend toward expressing these immaterial needs and these values quite openly. In this we echo the Victorian era.

The enormous Victorian outpouring of cards, verse, embroidered, painted, and printed sentiment are appreciated once again. At a time when we can reach the moon, talk to and even see the other side of the world (or inside the human body), we've come to appreciate anew the beauty in a clear stream, a fresh cup of coffee and a warm muffin, or a handmade card from a friend. Happy thought, isn't it, that this very evening you can be that friend!

[While Elly Sienkiewicz's talent and inspiration might derive from an earlier era, she herself appears to be forecasting the future. In 1997, if the American Quilter's Society had entitled her book *Applique Paper Memories* instead of *Applique Paper Greetings*, Elly would be considered a pioneer in the scrapbooking industry. The fact that she was nominated for the prestigious Primedia award for the best new book of 1998 indicates how well her applique designs and card making philosophy crossed over from fabric to paper.

The book has been reprinted in its entirety with two exceptions: Eight new scrapbooking pages may be found on pages 4–11 and more colorful illustrations have been added.–Ed.]

Quiltmaking + Greeting Cards = Scrapbooking

Modern scrapbooking is all the rage as scrapbookers explore the joys of artful memorabilia presentation. But though the passion "to scrapbook" blossoms contagiously, no one claims it is new. It is the latest chapter in album-making, a centuries-long story of artistic sensibility intertwined with sentiment.

By definition, albums are "collections on a theme." When we think of the more common albums, we think of paper ephemera – photos, post-cards, invitations, menus, tickets. But albums are more. They are the stuff of our fondest memories – the childhood ritual of collecting autographs in albums, the quiet pastime of making stamp albums, evenings spent pouring over old photo albums, the dreamy listening to the record albums of our youth.

Scrapbooking

Fig. 1. *BALTIMORE BASKET OF FLOWERS, 14" x 14", designed by Elly Sienkiewicz and stitched by Elly and Yvonne Von Nieda, 1992. The bouquet is cut out of a fusible-backed chintz, then heat-bonded to the background and edge-blanket-stitched.*

Fig. 2. *HELPMEETS, 14" x 14", pair of boat-tailed grackles by Elly Sienkiewicz, 1997. Grape arbor done in* broderie perse. *Both the print's outside cut edge and the interior design are finely blanket stitched and encrusted with varied embroidery.*

I n the current quilt revival we've rediscovered diverse antique Album Quilts (Signature Albums, Legacy Albums, Baltimore Albums). These quilt albums, too, present collections on a theme. As a quiltmaker, I came to album quilts first and then to melding cloth and cards, and finally to scrapbooking.

Like so many modern quiltmakers, my first traditional quilt was a sampler quilt. Samplers (a collection of different blocks) are of course a kind of album quilt. In 1983 I fell in love with the most famous album quilts, those made mid-nineteenth century, in and around Baltimore City, Maryland. By 1996, eleven of my eighteen books had been published. All were on album quilts and appliqué; so to some, when I taught and wrote about greeting card making techniques it seemed a departure! But a new use for modern technology had made an inspiring connection between cloth and paper for me, even as – through the album quilts – I explored one antique needlework technique and then another.

My cloth/paper connection came from studying chintzwork – an appliqué style in antebellum album quilts. In chintzwork, motifs (usually flora or fauna) are cut out of a chintz print and rearranged onto blocks or into larger scale designs to be appliquéd down to form the top for medallion-centered quilts. The engraved printed detail made these quilts ornate, destined to become heirlooms.

Even more ornate is *broderie perse* appliqué where chintz cutouts are blanket stitched to background cloth, then further embroidered within the print. The appliqués literally become "encrusted with embroidery." *The Victorian Encyclopedia of Needlework* (a reprint of the nineteenth-century original from Dover) notes that the chintz cutouts are to be pasted to the background cloth. It even gives the reader a recipe for the glue!

Because it is not as complex, chintzwork appliqué adapts very well to scrapbooking. A modern blessing – iron-on fusible bonding webs – eliminate the need for glue, and we can even "stitch" the edges of the paper appliqué cutouts with inked embellishment.

One evening I wanted to make an anniversary card for a friend in the quiltmaking industry. This was a big anniversary, so I made an oversized card – a basket of good wishes made by fusing fabric to card stock. It was such fun! Flowers – fused to paper – opened as mini-cards upon the card's base bouquet, each flower offering a wish. I used a woven print for the basket and made a fold-out support for the back so the card could stand, displayed. That was the beginning of such fun!

Each of us has, of course, made cards as a schoolchild. Discovering cloth fused to paper had opened childhood's promise into card-making – and now scrapbooking – as an artform! Years ago I was pulled to the Victorian greeting cards, so beautiful they'd been carefully preserved for 150 years and handed down to us. Many were sweetly sentimental, beautifully detailed, and marvels of paper engineering with their clever dimension and movable parts. It was exciting to explore all the details of cloth on paper through greeting cards – in all the richness of their construction and embellishment possibilities.

That exploration resulted in this book about cloth-on-paper appliqués. It focuses – in the main – on greeting cards. The current explosion of scrapbooking points to a whole new arena for using the skills and techniques explored in such depth in the following chapters.

In 2003 I received a wonderful honor as a quiltmaker: the Silver Star Award, presented annually by Quilts, Inc., to one who has been a significant influence on the contemporary quilt world. At the award ceremony, I was presented with an album of letters and notes from people commending my work as a quilt-maker and teacher. No ordinary album, this was a work of art – *a scrapbooked album*. The scrapbook's function was to present mementos of the award ceremony, The Silver Star Salute, along with the dozens of notes sent to me in care of Quilts, Inc., when they announced that I would receive the award.

Libby Lehman, a well-known quilter, had taken the lead in the scrapbooking, decorating the album with fancy papers and cutouts, ribbons, and other embellishments. When I thanked her she explained enthusiastically, "I just love scrapbooking!" Up till then I'd merely been an onlooker to scrapbooking.

Scrapbooking is the twenty-first century's term for a revered nineteenth-century craft, the making of Ladies' Albums. Scrapbooking is really another Victorian art revived, for the mid-nineteenth century was not only the heyday of the album quilt, it was also the era of the Ladies' Album – beautiful handmade books, individually created and filled with decorative illustrations and uplifting writings. Ladies' Albums, and photograph albums later in the era – were kept in parlors where they served as conversation pieces for hostess and visitor. For a family they taught about shared values and times past; they included pressed plants, poetry, memorabilia of places visited, stories, and artwork.

It was proposed that this book should be updated with a chapter on scrapbooking. Intrigued, I found several fine books on

Scrapbooking

scrapbooking at my bookstore. Their basic instructions need no repetition here. The simple techniques include using:

- premade photo mattes
- decorative-edged scissors
- straight-line paper cutters
- corner punches
- fancy lettering
- templates and die-cuts
- cutouts from photos
- decorative papers and printed borders
- premade pages and all the accessories currently available at craft and scrapbooking stores

Most modern scrapbooks present the sort of subject matter we whip out our cameras to record: birthdays, schooldays, graduations, marriage, anniversaries, holidays, vacations or a special trip. They are a way of collecting, presenting, and preserving our memories – like album quilts themselves. Like our quilts and the ladies' albums of yesteryear, they can be beautiful.

More and more quilters are discovering scrapbooking. But quilters have an edge that other scrapbookers may not possess. They can dip into the designs of quiltmaking for scrapbooking. Paper appliqué, or fabric on paper, can easily and elegantly enhance scrapbooking.

But there's more to scrapbooking than design, there's camaraderie. Scrapbookers, like quilters, often work in small groups, sometimes with a teacher. Like quiltmaking, scrapbooking helps build community in a fast-paced, impersonal world.

TOP LEFT. Grandma's Blooms, made by Earlina Scott, 2005. Pattern on page 187.

MIDDLE & BOTTOM LEFT. Made by Betty Alderman ©2005. Photo credit: Katja Sienkiewicz.

Betty Alderman ©2005.

RIGHT. *Apple Tree, made by Earlina Scott, ©2005. Enlarge pattern by photocopying or scanning to size needed.*

Scrapbook Gallery

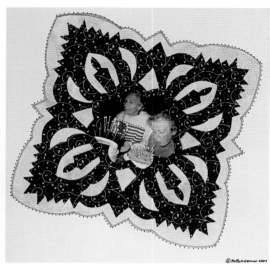

Scrapbook pages made by Betty Alderman ©2005.

ABOVE. *Patterns for box, page 69, cake, page 88, and lettering, page 184.*

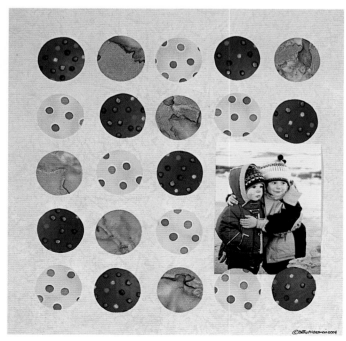

Scrapbook pages made by Betty Alderman ©2005.

How to Use This Book

Appliqué Paper Greetings uses a readily available sewing notion — webbed, fusible, plastic bonding — to attach fabric to paper. This technique joins two dynamic handwork traditions, paper craft and appliqué. The result is contemporary folk art. This wedding of two such familiar and easily usable materials is sure to become the craft marriage of the century. Its creative potential is enormous! This marriage benefits us on another level. In today's fast-paced era, the making of a greeting card nourishes our more contemplative and deliberate side. The comfortable and homey feeling of the card making process encourages us to visit with our past traditions, our present tastes, and with that very person whom we intend to greet and give a gift. Card making can serve one's need for independence, for creativity, and for quieting the soul. *Appliqué Paper Greetings* makes creating cards readily learnable as well as utterly delightful!

How Appliqué Paper Greetings Is Organized

Appliqué Paper Greetings teaches all about card making — what cards are, what they do, and the design and editorial approaches that make cards successful. The book is organized as a workbook with sequential lessons. With it, you can teach yourself and others how to make cloth-on-paper cards and mailable gift greetings. In Part One, "Getting Started" supplies and tools are enumerated along with important information about paper, cloth, marking pens, fusible bonding webs, techniques for bonding cloth to paper, and pattern transfer. The workbook lessons follow in Part Two. The lessons assume that you have read all the methods and materials in "Getting Started." They list only special supplies and

techniques needed beyond the basics.

Part Two is called "The Heart and Hand: Card Lessons." These eight lessons build on each other. Beginning with the simplest of cards, the cut-out design motif itself, the lessons move on to postcards and folded cards, dimensional cards, pop-up cards, cards that contain gifts, and greetings that go beyond the traditional gift of a card and can serve as gifts themselves. Ribbon flowers and other embellishments are covered, as are Techno-fancies made with either a simple, old-fashioned sewing machine, or a contemporary one. Part Three is "The Pattern Section." Here you'll find additional patterns, templates, and inspiration for your own original appliqués on cloth or cards.

Materials for Making Appliquéd Paper Greetings

In card making the choice of materials combines with artwork techniques and editorial approaches. Cloth and paper each burst with possibilities. Combined, their potential is endless! Bonding fabric to paper goes beyond construction paper, card stock, Bristol board, butcher paper, shelf paper, or art paper. Fabric can be bonded to ready-made paper products as well. Gift boxes can be ornamented with fused fabric. Betty Alderman, a guest designer for this book, even began a village of houses made of fabric fused to 5"–6" boxes. Fabric can be bonded to the oak tag of an accordion file for a quick and easy organizer. Fabric can also be bonded to commercial wrapping paper, gift bags, and paper mailers for gift giving. Wooden things and wood composites manufactured into boxes, clipboards, etc., can also be ornamented with fused cloth. Beyond cloth and paper, beyond the artwork and editorial processes, hovers the most important ingredient of all — magic that comes from you. Another word for this magic is creativity. Happily, it can be encouraged and even learned.

Observing Styles & Trends to Inspire Creativity

Once you have discovered how to do a craft, then you can begin to fertilize your creativity. The lessons in *Appliqué Paper Greetings* expand your explorations. In addition, researching consumer trends (in card shops, office supply stores, department stores, advertisements, magazines, libraries) will nourish your creativity. Media and the market place pitch consumers a dizzying display of styles. Certain ones strike a popular chord and when pushed, emerge as fads. But fads can fizzle fast. If you catch a cresting fad, you certainly may be able to use it successfully; but a surer tact is to watch for and use trends, longer lasting general directions.

For decades now American country has touched a responsive chord among consumers. The well-loved country trend is broadly based in our history and in our sense of self. It sings not only of hearth and home, but also of who we were, and who we hope to become. American country evokes a quieter, slower time, when solid values reigned and the importance of the individual loomed large. The American element in the country style carries the untarnished mystique of this country as a grand experiment — what Abe Lincoln named "the last, best hope of earth." Similarly rooted in our history is the current popularity of Victoriana. It became popular at the beginning of the Industrial Age. Now in the Age of Communications, uncertainties

beset us. Perhaps because of this, last century's cultural adjustment to changing times increasingly compels our attention and appeals to our taste. Can you see both these long-holding trends, the American country and Victoriana, in this book's card models? These two trends are sure bets through yet another century's turn!

FOLK ART: WHATEVER THE HAND SHALL DO, IT SHALL BE GUIDED BY THE HEART

Traditional folk art motifs inspire many of the book's cards and crafts. For clarity each of the initial lessons demonstrates its techniques with models on a heart theme, sometimes with another motif which is often the heart and hand. Because they are among our most beloved folk art motifs, these heart-and-hand models hold wide appeal. By repeating these motifs but changing the card-making methods, the lesson by lesson distinctions in technique become clear. This repetitious format automatically tucks the mechanics of card making into your toolbox. Why not work your way through the lessons for an overview? Then with a wealth of possibilities at hand, take on the "The Pattern Section." Make any of this book's pictured models, then create a home card shop, full of your own designs! You may discover magic in these cards as well as in yourself!

Appliqué Paper Greetings delivers a method for cloth and paper craft right to your easy chair. Its simple expression brims with vitality. Share the process with family and friends. Witness the speed at which novices become innovators, pushing the craft to new limits. Beyond recreation and self-expression, folk art passes on traditional culture. In this spirit let's recall the origins of our heart-and-hand theme before beginning Part One.

The Heart and the Hand

"Hand and Heart Shall Never Part — When This You See, Remember Me." By this charming verse, written on a mid-nineteenth-century paper love token, some swain entreated a now forgotten maiden. The heart and hand image is as American as quiltmaking. The heart-and-hand motif conjures up folk art images: cookie cutters, appliqués, valentines. Where does it come from? How far back does it go? The heart and the hand as separate symbols, it turns out, go back as far as human record. They have been found painted on cave walls by prehistoric humans for whom, we believe, hearts symbolized life, and hands, an attempt at power over the spirit of the vital animal prey.

For Western Civilization, the heart came to mean romantic love, devotion, piety, charity, friendship, and, if you are Scandinavian, good luck. From throwing down the gauntlet — surrendering in the Middle Ages — the hand may have become a symbol entwined with romance by the seventeenth century in England, for example. In that time and place, a gift of heart-decorated gloves might have been accompanied by the verse: *"If that from Glove you take the letter G, Then Glove is love and that I send to Thee."* My Victorian grandmother explained that even in her own youth, coy suitors sought to steal a lady's glove, giving cause to see her again for its return. "It made me angry," she said, and then confided that coquettish damsels, too, might casually drop a glove, happily anticipating its return. Hands are reached out in friendship, offered in succor, and given in marriage. That the heart-and-hand motif occurs so frequently in our own folk art today reflects the strength of its appeal. But where did that motif come from?

The Shaker motto is "Hands to work, hearts to God." I have seen pictured a nineteenth-century Shaker paper heart award, given a student perhaps. But while paper-cut heart-and-hand love tokens come to us from the last century, they are not connected just to the Shakers. As a decorative motif, the heart and hand seems to have originated as an Odd Fellow emblem. It symbolized this fraternal brotherhood's tenet: "Whatsoever the hand finds to do, the heart should go forth in unison, and render the tasks doubly sweet by its savor of affection." This symbol for service and the spirit in which it is delivered is certainly an appealing sentiment. Today it seems to translate broadly as loyalty, dependability, trustworthiness, or simply, friendship. Perhaps just because the heart and hand are both such dear old symbols, they speak to us each in our own way. Above all, though, they suggest goodness, affection, loyal friendship, and love. They constitute about as universally evocative a two-shape symbol as card makers can hope to explore.

Getting Started

Introducing

Paper Appliqué

Appliqué is a sewing term meaning to sew decorative cloth patches onto background material. These same patches can be attached to paper by a fusible plastic bonding. They can also then be sewn easily by machine to the background cards. However, they do not even have to be sewn! They are well bonded by the fusible. This makes cloth onto paper the easiest appliqué of all.

FUSIBLE FACTS

An iron-on fusible is a thin web of plastic that, when sandwiched between fabric and paper (or between fabric and fabric) and pressed with heat, bonds the two together. The concept is so simple that you could use one layer of a thin plastic bag to do the trick. But melted, that plastic film is messy and hard to handle. More recent improvements protect the iron from a mess and us from unwanted frustration and cleanup.

Modern fusible bonding webs are backed with protective paper which protects the iron from the melting plastic. This improvement has been so great that manufacturers have dubbed their products with blithe names such as Wonder-Under® and Aleene's Hot-Stitch Fusible Web®, or simply descriptive names like Heat 'n Bond® or Therm O Web®. Improved by the paper backing, these fusibles are a breeze to use and come in different thicknesses for different weights of fabric. For cards, use the original, regular, or lightweight fusible bonding web. By and large we will be bonding shirt (sheeting) weight fabric to paper: A heavy duty bonding is too thick for this fabric. Fusible bondings come wrapped on bolts and are sold where cloth is sold. Because excessive handling separates the web from the paper, store fusible yardage around a tube (from a roll of paper towels?), a recycled fabric bolt sleeve, or fold it flat and pack it in a file folder.

WHICH SIDE OF THE FUSIBLE IS WHICH?

Paper Side. The paper covering is transparent and smooth, so pattern transfer is easy. Place the pattern (a heart motif, for instance) right side up on the work surface. Position the fusible (paper side up) over the pattern. Through the paper, trace the heart in pencil (Fig. 1). Do not cut the drawn heart out of the fusible. Instead cut a swatch about ½" bigger than the heart all around. You won't cut the heart out as a separate shape until the fusible has been bonded to the fabric.

The Plastic Side. The webbed plastic side feels rough and is the raw fusing material. Place the appliqué fabric wrong side up on a hard ironing surface. (Note: A cardboard fabric bolt sleeve makes an ideal, hard ironing board.) Position the heart swatch of fusible with its rough side against the fabric's wrong side. The iron, safe from mess, will now glide over the protective paper (Fig. 2).

HOW IS THE FABRIC BONDED & THEN FUSED TO THE PAPER?

Different brands give various directions. One maker advises a hot iron for several seconds, for example; another specifies a moderate iron for one to three seconds. Always read your fusible's package directions, then pretest. The following directions are basic:

- Using a hot, dry iron, press the swatch's plastic web surface to the wrong side of the fabric (Fig. 2).
- Cut the fused heart out of the fabric, along the drawn line. Allow it to cool for a few seconds before lifting off the protective paper.
- Having difficulty separating the paper? *Solution:* Make a slight tearing motion at the heart's cut edge. It will tear the paper, but not the fabric threads.
- Appliquéing the heart to the card: Position the heart patch (plastic-coated side down) against the card. To ensure that this ornament doesn't shift, dab glue onto its wrong (fusible) side with a glue stick and

paste the patch down. (This glue spot secures the patch for bonding. Then it simply dries out in the bonding process.)

- Use a clean sheet of paper as a pressing cloth to protect the card from the iron. Heat press not just the heart, but the whole card. (Were you to press just the area of the heart, it would warp the card.) *Success Tip:* Iron to bond quickly. You can redo it if the bond does not hold. Lingering too long with too hot an iron causes problems (Fig. 3).

PATTERN TRANSFER METHODS

There are multiple ways of getting the appliqué shape onto the fused fabric. As you work your way through the lessons, you'll find yourself using each method at one time or another.

Pattern Transfer Method #1. Trace the pattern to the fusible first (Fig. 1). Then iron the pattern swatch to the fabric (Fig. 2).

Pattern Transfer Method #2. Fuse the fabric first, then use a template to draw the pattern shape onto the protective paper (Fig. 4, p. 20).

Pattern Transfer Method #3. Fuse the fabric first, then cut out a shape freehand, double on-the-fold. One holiday season, I used this method to make quantities of the Christmas Tree postcards. It worked wonderfully and was more fun than repeating the exact same tree each time (Fig. 5, p. 20).

Pattern Transfer Method #4. Cut a shape out of the fabric print itself. What a wealth of gorgeous fabrics we can select from these days! Many conversation prints have realistic motifs that can be cut right out of fabric. Of course, you would have fused the fabric

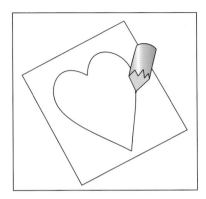

Fig. 1. *Pattern Transfer Method #1a. Trace the heart shape onto the paper side of the fusible.*

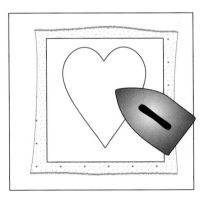

Fig. 2. *Pattern Transfer Method #1b. Place the marked fusible over the cloth: plastic side of the fusible to the wrong side of the cloth. Iron the paper covering to bond the two together, cut the fused heart out.*

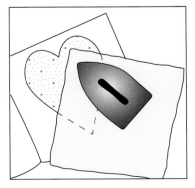

Fig. 3. *Pattern Transfer Method #1c. Using a press cloth, iron the whole card to fuse the cloth heart to the paper. If you iron only the appliquéd part of the card, the paper will warp.*

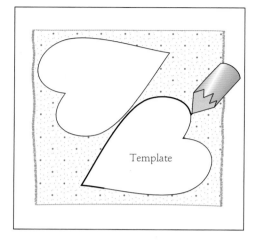

Fig. 4. *Pattern Transfer Method #2. Drawing a repeated shape on pre-fused fabric is efficient.*

Fig. 5. *Pattern Transfer Method #3. To cut a shape out of fused fabric: hold a folded paper template over the cloth's fold. Or, cut the shape freehand, double-on-the-fold.*

before cutting out such a printed image.

PHENOMENAL PAPER

Paper is familiar, ordinary material. We use it in quantity and easily throw it away. But paper is also an ingenious material. An ancient discovery, it is phenomenally versatile! Glorious in its spectrum of colors, weights, and textures, paper is an equal partner with cloth in the many possibilities for paper greetings. Like elegant fabric, fine paper, too, is expensive. If we want to make cards in large quantities, or plan to make them with children, we need to explore not only the special properties of paper, but also the most economical sources for everyday card making. Splurges are all too tempting. My favorite art store splurge papers are white Bristol board and packages of colored Strathmore "Art Paper" in the 9" x 12" and 12" x 18" sizes. (Note that the color selection varies from one size package to the next.) Increasingly quilt and craft shops and office supply stores are carrying boxes of colored Strathmore folded notes with matching envelopes. These are ideal for this book's cards.

Paper Weight. The paper most familiar to us is called 20-pound white. This means that a ream of this white paper weighs twenty pounds. This is the paper American businesses run on, the paper used in copy machines, and the common paper used for flyers. The weight of the paper is measured by grams per square meter (gsm2). Average paper weighs from 80 to 125 gsm2. Tissue paper is lighter, while card weight paper (225 gsm2 and up) is heavier. If the paper weighs more than 500 gsm2, it is called board, hence the origin of the terms Bristol board or cardboard.

For card making we need the heavier papers from card stock right up through

Bristol board. A good place to buy card stock is from your printer or local paper distributor. (See your Yellow Pages.) Both have sample books displaying a wide variety of papers for you to look over at better than retail prices. For efficiency, have the printer cut paper to your preferred card size. It costs pennies and sets you up for great productivity. I have the printer cut quantities of 8½" x 11" red card stock sheets into thirds for postcards and into halves for larger flat cards or fold-over note cards. The lessons will often call for red card stock, but you should choose your own favorite color. Printers sometimes have left-over stock with matching envelopes ordered for weddings or other fancy occasions. These miscellaneous papers are often bargains. On the other hand, you can purchase elegant boxed sets of blank cards (plain with color borders or deckle-edged) at stationery stores. These boxed sets, appliquéd by you, would make someone a lovely, but not inexpensive gift. Paper is clearly popular these days and widely available in a peppy array of colors, sizes, prints, and plains. Card and paper stores display an enticing rainbow of sheets matched with envelopes. Quality art stores have sumptuous papers. Even drug stores have construction paper, though it is a little lightweight for cards. A pleasant mail-order source for quantity paper purchases is Paper Direct at 1-800-A-PAPERS.

FABULOUS FABRIC & INVITING EMBELLISHMENTS

Embellishments: Fusible-bonding purchased by the yard is essential for making paper greetings. Beyond this, your scrap-bag starts you with plenty of cloth for making this book's cards and gifts. If looking through the galleries inspires you and sets you yearning for specific prints and colors, buy cottons or poly-cottons as standard supplies. In addition, any other cloth — fur scraps, woolens, rayons, silks, velveteens, laces, decorator cottons, novelty prints, plaids, stripes, or polka-dots, even recycled clothing — will do. When you go on to embellishments, begin with ribbons large and small, then think of glitter, glitter glue, liquid embroidery paints, metallic and paper confetti, sequins of all shapes and

Kid-Appeal Memo

Great News! The most convenient and inexpensive way to purchase quantity blank cards for working with children is to buy packages of file cards. File cards are a good postcard weight. They come plain or ruled, white or in colors. They take ink, glue, and fused fabric well. Best of all their precut sizes fit standard envelopes! Betty Alderman who made so many of this book's paper greeting models, designed the majority of them on the large size file cards (4⅞" x 8") folded as note cards. File cards should be a standard supply for all card makers. The last lesson has instructions for making envelopes for those cards that are irregular sizes.

sizes, and buttons. If collages appeal to you, consider artificial flowers, cocktail picks, twigs, feathers, stamps, pieces taken from magazine copy and photos, and even fancy, printed wrapping paper, origami paper, and tissues. I've even tucked tiny seashells into slits in cards, roses into appliquéd hands as well as sachets, tea bags, bubble bath packets, and dollar bills into willing paper card pockets!

Finishing Touches: A handmade, home-made-looking card brings a smile of forgotten pleasure to those who hold it. Making a professional one impressive enough to sell in boutique card shops for up to two-figure prices feels great, too! Finishing touches often give that professional look. Many of the boutique cards feature the third dimension and a found object. Richly textured materials, varied both to the eye and to the touch, are often incorporated. An easier boutique card touch is embellishing with ink. Study it on the cards pictured in color. I used gold or silver metallic ink from felt-tip pens (both bold and fine) for edging, shading with dots, and for drawing bows. Betty Alderman uses a fine or medium black, felt-tip pen. Skillfully, she dots in backgrounds, adds dotted dimension to folk art motifs, and shades with dots for realistic scene-setting details.

Setting Up a Work Area & Getting in Supplies

If you have a neat, clean, accessible workspace for card making, great! If not, there are solutions. When uncluttered surfaces for card making are scarce, try double-decker. A hollow-core door from the lumber yard makes my portable workspace. Sometimes I use it on my queen-size bed, sometimes I put it on top of two yellow plastic storage cubes placed at either end of my oak table desk. Sometimes I put it across the backs of two upholstered armchairs and sit on a kitchen stool. All of these work. This is my set-up: At one end of this door/table is a travel iron on an extension cord. A heavy cardboard (the back of a 12" x 18" art pad) protects the work surface for ironing on it, cutting on it with an art knife, or gilding the edge of cards. At the other end is the day's supply of paper and fabric, a coffee can with colored, felt-tip pens, gold and silver markers, gridded and steel rulers, mechanical pencils, art knives, a rotary cutter, and my jealously guarded paper and fabric scissors. A beige, plastic wastebasket is always below it. A flat, brown bag for saving fused scraps is taped to the handmade table above it. In a nearby room I keep an iron and ironing board set up, a tabletop paper cutter, shelves with books on quotes, verses, sampler inscriptions, and photocopy notebooks of favorite commercial greeting cards. Kept always in the same place are:

- Graph paper, sketch pad, reams of blank #20 white, stacks of precut, red card stock, art paper, white file cards held together by different sizes with rubber bands.
- Architectural circle templates, compass, a right-angle, hole punches.
- Drafting tape (used as a straight edge for inscribing cards). Removable adhesive tape (for temporarily pasting up layouts).
- Adhesives: Glue stick (permanent and removable), white glue, rubber cement.

When the card making day is done, I put all of the day's supplies away in a brown cardboard box and stand the door in a corner, well hidden behind a stationary door.

Speed-up Spot

MASS-PRODUCTION `A LA VALENTINE

Question: I want to make a dozen heart postcards for Valentine's day. Can I speed up the whole paper appliqué process?

Answer: Absolutely! The key thing to remember is that for mass production, it is always faster to fuse your fabric first and then transfer the pattern. So begin by fusing a fat quarter yard (18" x 22"). With this prepared yardage, use a sturdy template (Fig. 4, Pattern Transfer Method #2) to draw the heart onto the paper backing 12 times.

QUICK TEMPLATE MAKING

To be drawn around repeatedly, a template must be plastic or a heavy enough paper to have a stable edge. Save yourself time by making up a batch of rugged templates all at once.

- From the Pattern Section, trace or photocopy the pattern shapes you will use a lot.
- To make a sturdy heart template using a photocopied template, for example: Roughly cut out a swatch containing the photocopy of a heart. The swatch should be about ½" bigger all-around than the heart's outline.
- Using a glue stick or rubber cement, paste the heart swatch to poster board. *Recycle Suggestion:* For template material, use the side of a cereal box, a plastic gallon jug, the cardboard from a package of stockings, a cardboard express mail envelope, or a used file folder.
- Cutting right on the heart pattern line, cut your shape out of the poster board. Its relative thickness makes a heart template that can be traced around quickly.

FAST VALENTINES: CUTTING FREEHAND ON-THE-FOLD

Even speedier than tracing around a template, is to cut the hearts out freehand, double on-the-fold. If this seems too quick and cavalier, try this almost-freehand transfer method: To repeat the exact same heart multiple times, cut the paper template on-the-fold. Now simply hold the template (pressing steadily) over the fused fabric's fold while you cut around it. No drawing is needed!

ASSEMBLY LINE PRODUCTION

Henry Ford usually gets the credit for assembly-line production. His original automobile factory earned him this reputation. But who knows where he got the idea? Perhaps it was helping his father with the task of first cutting hay, making haystacks, and then fencing them. Or perhaps it was when he watched his wife do patchwork or put mincemeat up in canning jars and then label them. Any farmer, cook, or craftsperson knows that the way to produce large quantities is to do the beginning step for all the units first, then the second step, and so on until, in this case, all the Valentine postcards are signed, addressed, stamped, and ready to send!

Instant Info

PAPER SURFACE AND GRAIN

Paper can be handmade or machine-made, sized (surface-coated) or unsized. Because sized paper is less absorbent, ink does not bleed easily on it. Unsized paper is called waterleaf. Machine-made papers have a grain because the fibers settle in one direction — the way the mold, a belt, moves. The grain affects the way paper rolls and folds.

Testing a Paper for Its Grain Direction. To learn whether the grain runs perpendicular or horizontal in a piece of paper, curl it first in one direction, then in the other. Press the rolled sheet gently with one hand to see which direction it bends the easiest. It will do this when the bend parallels the direction of the grain:

- This diagram shows a paper sheet with a vertical grain (Fig. A).
- The sheet doesn't bend as easily from top to bottom (Fig. B).
- The sheet bends more easily from left to right because the curl follows the direction of the grain (Fig. C).
- Paper tears straighter along the direction of the grain than it does across the grain (Fig. D).

In card making, what if we need to fold the paper against its grain? In Lesson 2, we'll cover a neat trick called "scoring" the paper, so that it folds cleanly wherever you want it to, regardless of the grain.

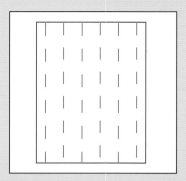

Fig. A.

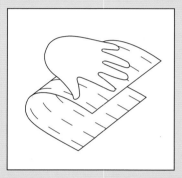

Fig. B.

Fig. C.

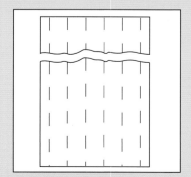

Fig. D.

Design Themes

When you need a card for a special occasion, or want to decorate a ready-made gift, consider these basic design themes for inspiration:

- Fabric Predominant. Using the fabric's design (including lace and ribbon) to find a paper greeting theme (Fig. 6).
- Motif Predominant. Using shapes traditionally associated with the card occasion may lead you to a paper greeting concept (Fig. 7).
- Editorial (Words) Predominant. Most card occasions are associated with simple words, greetings, or phrases. Sometimes a poem, verse, or bit of doggerel will give you your paper greeting idea (Fig. 8).

You'll see examples of these design themes in the cards pictured in this book. As you proceed through the lessons now, ask yourself what design each one uses. (You'll find the lessons are heavy on the motif theme!) If you can conjure up related but different themes for your cards, then every lesson will inspire your pleasurable pursuit of Paper Greetings!

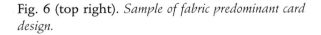

Fig. 6 (top right). *Sample of fabric predominant card design.*

Fig. 7 (center right). *Sample of motif predominant card design.*

Fig. 8 (bottom right). *Sample of editorial (words) predominant card design.*

Part Two

The Heart and Hand:
Card Lessons

Take a shape, any appealing shape. How many things can you do with it to make a nifty card? Or better yet, don't take just any shape. Take that most universally loved of all our symbols, the heart. The following lessons are recipes for making a heart, a heart with a hand, or another motif, into a card. Card recipe lessons follow. Try them! While hearts and hands dominate the card lesson motifs, the artwork you will learn applies to dozens of card designs. You'll quickly grasp the potential of this fabric-on-cloth medium and make it your own. Your cards and greetings for gifts will soar far beyond the bounds defined by *Appliqué Paper Greetings*.

Left. *Photo credit: Elly Sienkiewicz.*

The Cut-out Shape Becomes the Card

- *Cards: Valentine-shaped Cards*
- *Techniques: Drawing a Folk-Art Heart, Cutting Out a Shaker Heart, Paper Cut Flush with Fused Fabric, Paper Cut Bordering the Fabric, Edge-Gilding, Envelope Seal, Mirror Image Motifs on Cards Hinged by a Fold, Interior Cuts, Additional Embellishments*
- *Editorial Element: Adding an Inscription, Line Texture, Creating Anticipation*
- *Gift Greetings: Hanging Ornament, Bookmark, Note Cards*
- *Special Materials: Standard red card stock, felt-tip pens with gold metallic ink (fine and bold)*

A card shaped like another object pleases us. It's different. Most cards today are squares or rectangles. Like cans of beans in a grocery store, cards march repetitiously across a store's shelves. The present echoes the past, though, and object-shaped cards are coming back. Victorian designers delighted in cards cut into decorative shapes. Often the shape was an everyday motif such as a shoe, a tea cup, a heart. Victorian industry was versatile. Its entrepreneurs were excited about what machines in factories could make. Even greeting cards could be mass produced! We feel that enthusiasm still in the generosity of die-cut cards reproduced from that era. Today children who make Valentine's cards still love the simple cut-out hearts. They also abound in the inexpensive, manufactured Valentines youngsters give secretly to classmates. Even the simple outline of the heart entices us. Chocolate hearts, sugar cookie hearts warming sweetly in the oven, tarnished silver locket hearts. Let's experiment with hearts cut double on-the-fold and see what deliciousness we can cook up!

A Folk-Art Heart

When hearts are cut on-the-fold, the design drawn on the top surface is mirrored by the bottom surface. This mirrored shape is connected along the fold. Easy! Some hearts even have names and are made by formulas. One such is the Folk-Art Heart. The following fail-proof formula makes a curvaceous Folk-Art Heart. Try it!

- Fold a 4" square of graph paper in half, taking the right side over the left (Fig. 1-1A).
- On the outer layer, draw two 2" circles, one sitting above the other (Fig. 1-1B).

- Next, draw a heavy line from the where the top circle touches the fold, up and around the top circle, then down the left side of the bottom circle, tapering it in to touch the fold (Fig. 1-1C).
- Now cut the complete heart out, double on-the-fold. Cut along the drawn line. Begin at the bottom point on-the-fold, and cut up to the top of the heart, right into where the drawn line intersects the fold again (Fig. 1-1D).
- The result is a flawless Folk-Art Heart!

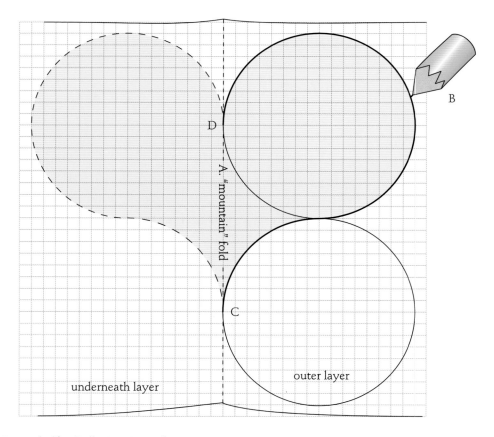

Fig. 1-1A–D. *Draw half a Folk-Art Heart from two circles, then cut it out double on-the-fold.*

A Shaker Heart

Among the most graceful of hearts is the proud, high-shouldered Shaker Heart, steeply narrowing to a point (Fig. 1-2). While there is no magical formula for making a Shaker Heart, we observe that ¼ of its height is in its shoulders, ¾ is in its finial. The best way to learn the shape is to practice cutting it double on-the-fold. The delicately tapered Folk-Art Heart looks best to me as an ornament mounted on a card. The sturdy Shaker Heart looks appealing as a heart-shaped, cut-out card. We appreciate its almost perfect harmony of proportion. So classic is the Shaker Heart that you can inscribe it with the simplest greeting or make it into a number of small gifts that can be mailed in an envelope.

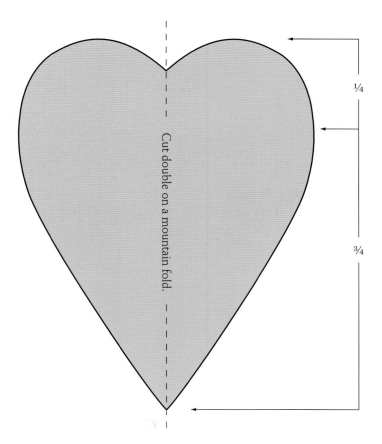

Cut double on a mountain fold.

¼

¾

Fig. 1-2. *A classic Shaker Heart.*

* ARTWORK RECIPE 1:

A Heart-Shaped, Cut-Out Card

Review Fusible Facts in Part One: "Getting Started." As needed, refer back to those basics for subsequent lessons.

- Trace template 1 (a Shaker Heart) onto fusible, plastic bonding web. Cut this heart out on a swatch ½" bigger all-around than the heart shape itself (Fig. 1-3A).
- Fuse this heart-drawn fusible to the wrong side of the chosen fabric (Fig. 1-3B).
- Next cut the heart shape out of the fused fabric. Peel off the fusible protective paper. What you've made is a cheery iron-on heart patch.

- By ironing, heat-bond the heart patch to the red card stock. Caution: Always use a paper press cloth to avoid marring the card and other heartbreaks.
- Cut the card stock out on the same line as the cut fabric edge (Fig. 1-4).

Fig. 1-4. *Cloth-covered card cut from card stock on the same line as the fused heart.*

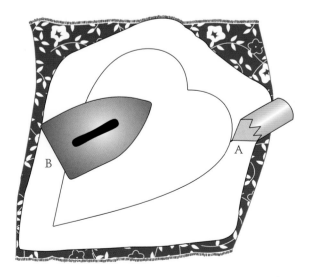

Fig. 1-3A&B. *Trace template onto fusible, plastic bonding web.*

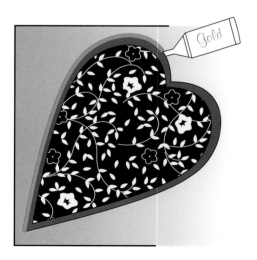

Fig. 1-5. *Embellishment option: leave a ¹⁄₁₆" margin to the card stock and gild its edge.*

Embellishment Option: Gilding the edge of the card. To gild the edge, change step #5 to read: Cut the card stock $\frac{1}{16}$" beyond the cut fabric edge (Fig. 1-5). To gild this exposed edge, place the cut-out heart over cardboard to protect the work surface. Use a metallic gold felt-tip (bold) pen for the gilding. If the pen has not been used recently, shake it to mix its ink, then press the point down momentarily on the cardboard to start the ink flowing. (This pressing to fill the pen tip with ink has to be done periodically. For safety, always do it away from the final artwork.) After testing the gold pen to get a feel for how fast the ink flows, hold its point against the cardboard as though you were tracing around the heart (Fig. 1-6). Then lean it firmly against the cut heart as you pull the pen towards you. The pen's edge will lay down a gleaming line along the cut outline of the paper heart. You become skilled at turning the heart to minimize lifting up the pen on its golden trip around this Valentine. Soon it is time to inscribe the card.

Fig. 1-6. Template 1. Back of the card, showing inscription in two pen widths and colors. The red card back has been edge-gilded and gold-dusted with pen dots to fill its margins.

Editorial Element: To tie the card together, use the same metallic gold, but fine-tipped, to write the card's brief traditional inscription (I love you! Be mine! Best wishes, Get well soon, please) on the card stock's fabric-free side. Add your personal message and then sign off in a Pigma Micron® .01 (or any ultra-fine) black pen. The switch from the decorative gold marker to a signing pen adds contrast, line weight texture, and interest. It leaves the golden inscription looking more professional.

*Envelope Size: This template 1 card fits a 4¾" x 6½" standard envelope. Address it with the same fine black signing pen. And why not seal its flap with a small fused heart (Fig. 1-7)? Envelopes peak your recipient's anticipation. Seize the opportunity! If pen work appeals to you, ornament that envelope with a gilt edging and a dusting of gold pen dots. Decorate that address! The recipient will open this envelope carefully, already knowing that it holds something special.

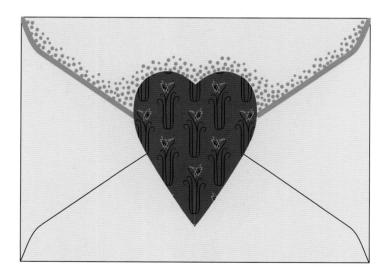

Fig. 1-7. *Ornament the envelope with gilt edging, a dusting of gold dots, and seal it with an elegant fused heart.*

Fig. 1-8. *Template 2.*

Fig. 1-9 (right). *Template 3. Make a set of calico Christmas tree hearts.*

Gift Greetings

Ornament

Make a smaller cloth card using Template 2 (Fig 1-8, p. 35). For a functional card, a kept object, use the heavier Bristol board rather than card stock. So that this heart can be hung, punch a hole directly below its inside point (Fig. 1-8, p. 35). Use a ⅛" punch. Art or office supply stores carry hole punches not only in the standard ¼" hole size, but also the smaller, more delicate ⅛" size. Tie a 10" length of ⅛" wide red satin ribbon through the hole and knot it again, about ⅓ of the way up (Fig. 1-8, p. 35). With the loop you've just made, this heart can be hung to send love, a wish to get well. Made at a smaller size with Template 3 (Fig. 1-9, p. 35), it could deck a Christmas tree. A nicely packaged set of red calico Christmas tree ornament hearts would make a charming holiday friendship gift.

Bookmark

Make a decorative interior cut in Template 4's smaller Shaker Heart. Cut it so that the shape can slip over a page (Fig. 1-10). This turns your greeting into a bookmark, an easily mailed remembrance.

INTERIOR CUTS

The best way is to cut the final shape out of the fused fabric (see Step #3, p. 32) before bonding it to Bristol board (Fig. 1-10). That way, the fabric won't interfere with a clean cutting of the card stock. After bonding the cloth to the card stock, cut the heart's outline with scissors, but always cut its interior lines with an art knife.

Accept this marker from a friend who is thinking of you, through this book's end!

Fig. 1-10. *Template 4. This bookmark slips over the page to hold your friend's place. It is a perfect card-as-gift to send just to say, "I'm thinking of you."*

MIRROR IMAGE SHAPE CARDS,
CUT-OUT DOUBLE, AND HINGED BY A FOLD

There are lots of other heart shapes for card making. Most of them are simply the lucky creation of cutting paper double on-the-fold. A number of heart templates are presented at the book's end in the "Pattern Section." For inspiration, browse there!

Doesn't surprise in a greeting card delight you? (Watch for a grin lighting up a card shopper's face. If he puts that card back and picks up another one, it's likely to have been surprise as much as sentiment that pleased him.) Even cleverness, when least expected, qualifies as surprise. Let's make two mirror-image, double heart cards. Each is hinged by placing the heart on a top fold or side fold. These simple plays on a heart shape aren't seen often. To me, they're fresh and innovative. All sorts of design motifs can be partially placed on a fold to make a hinged card. Enjoy the journey!

Fig. 1-11. *Fold a 4" x 8" rectangle of card stock in half lengthwise.*

Fig. 1-12. *Heart shape cut double on-the-fold.*

Cut a Mirror-Image Heart Out on a Side Fold

- Fold a 4" x 8" rectangle of red card stock in half lengthwise (Fig. 1-11).
- Cut out a fused fabric heart made from Heart Template 5 (Fig. 1-13, p. 38). (This particular heart's straight-sloping sides form a right-angle.)
- Fuse the Template 5 fabric heart to the top surface of the folded card stock. Place it so that the left side of the heart's taper lies on the fold, while its right side lies on the card's base.
- Cut the heart shape out, double, on-the-fold.

Editorial Element: Does the fabric you fused to the card's front suggest an interior inscription to you? Cloth sprigged with flowers, for example, might lead to: "Hearts and flowers always make me think of you!"

Gift Greeting

This particular card would also make a lovely blank card. To make a gift set of them, use Template 5 which fits a standard sized 5¼" x 4¼" envelope. Consider fusing elegant cream-background floral prints to rich cream card stock with off-white envelopes. With a shaded wire-edged French ribbon, tie a package of 10 of these cards and envelopes. Such a presentation of note cards would make a fine bread-and-butter present for a gracious hostess — or serve as a thoughtful token of affection for a friend who says she doesn't really want her birthday celebrated!

Cloth-covered Envelope

This cloth-covered envelope is the perfect size for Artwork Recipe 2's Side-opening Heart-shaped card. To make this envelope:

- From fused cloth, cut the envelope from the pattern in Fig. 1-14, p. 39.
- Heat-bond this envelope appliqué to red card stock (or shelf paper or lightweight brown wrapping paper).
- Cut the paper out on the lines of the fabric appliqué.
- Lay the cut but not yet folded envelope on the table, with the inside facing up.
- Following the fold lines marked on the template, score the four valley folds.
- Fold the left and right side flaps in first. Paint the lower half of the triangle's margins with rubber cement. Paint it on the outside of the envelope in about a ⅓" wide strip.
- Similarly, paint the inside of the bottom flap's margins with rubber cement. Allow a few seconds for the glue to get tacky.
- Fold up the bottom flap and press firmly to seal it against the overlapped side flaps.
- Slip in the folded heart card and tuck in the top back flap.

Variations: If you want to mail this card, you'll need to put on a self-stick mailing label. Or you may want to cut a stamp and address window into the envelope appliqué before you heat-bond it to paper.

hinge fold

Fig. 1-13. *Template 5. A side-opening heart makes a clever card.*

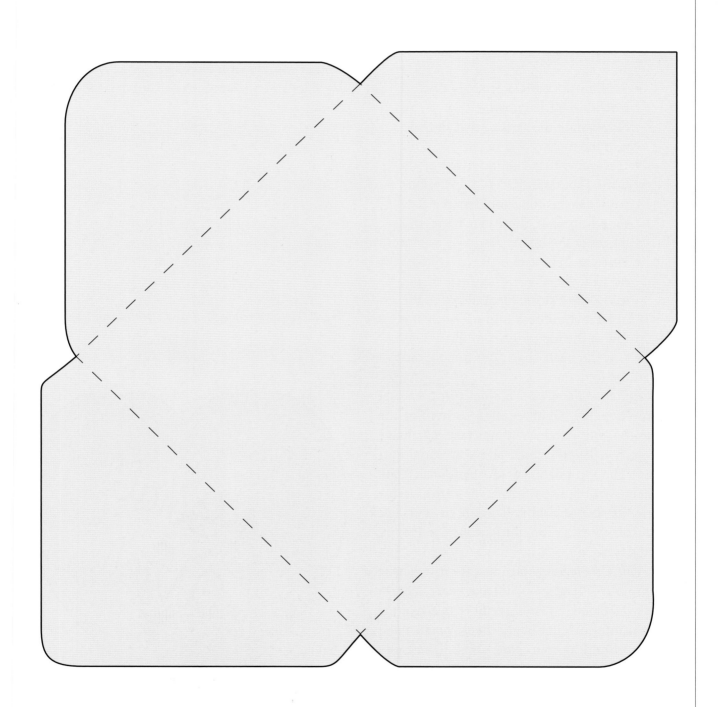

Fig. 1-14. *Cloth-covered envelope for Artwork Recipe 2: A Side-opening Heart Card.*

* ARTWORK RECIPE 3:

Cut Out a Mirror-Imaged Heart Double on a Bottom-Opening Fold

- Fold a 4¼" x 8¼" rectangle of card stock in half lengthwise (Fig. 1-15). Now rotate the card so that the fold is at the top.
- Cut out a fused fabric heart made from Template 6 (Fig. 1-16). (This particular heart's shoulders are flattened so that they can form the hinges at the fold.)
- Fuse the Template 6 (Fig. 1-16) fabric heart to the top surface of the folded card stock. Place it so that the heart's shoulders line up with the fold at the top of the card (Fig 1-17).
- Cut the heart shape out double on-the-fold.

Editorial Element: This card you've just made is petite, small enough to hold in the palm of your hand. Why not take advantage of its two layers which allow editorial surprise. The top might say "A small wish," and inside: "For big happiness!" The card's design (here, its size) should underscore its message. Sign off with a Congratulations! or Happy Birthday!

Gift Greeting: Try an interior cut to make Template 7 (Fig 1-20) into a heart wreath (Figs. 1-18 and 1-19). Remember to make the initial interior cuts in the heart patch itself before bonding it to card stock. The open wreath frames a heart space inside the card. Does this suggest other options to you? Perhaps a school photo portrait pasted beneath the frame, an inscribed phrase, or a sketched motif?

Embellishment Option: For other variations, consider ornamenting the wreath with fused flower cut-outs or twined ribbons. This is a card with potential! Keep it in mind when you learn about heavier card stock, scoring, and ribbon rosettes in upcoming lessons. But first we'll look at the humble postcard in Lesson 2.

Fig. 1-15. *Fold rectangle of card stock in half lengthwise.*

Fig. 1-16. *Template 6. A mirror-image heart cut-out double on-the-hinge.*

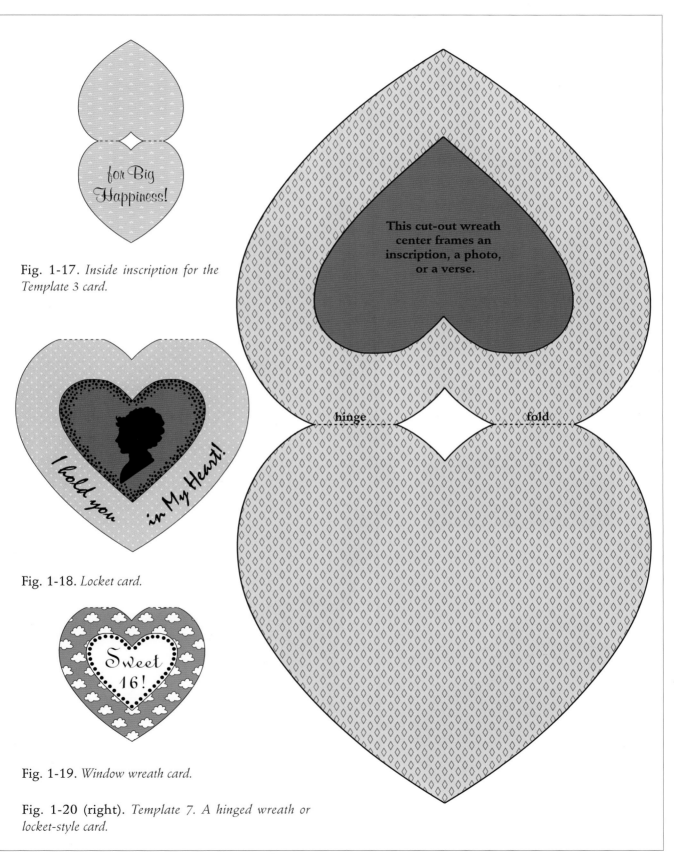

for Big Happiness!

Fig. 1-17. *Inside inscription for the Template 3 card.*

I hold you in My Heart!

Fig. 1-18. *Locket card.*

Sweet 16!

Fig. 1-19. *Window wreath card.*

Fig. 1-20 (right). *Template 7. A hinged wreath or locket-style card.*

This cut-out wreath center frames an inscription, a photo, or a verse.

hinge   fold

Card 1-3, below. *Made by Betty Alderman, © 1992.*

Card 1-1. *Made by Betty Alderman, © 1992.*

Card 1-2. *Made by Elly Sienkiewicz.*

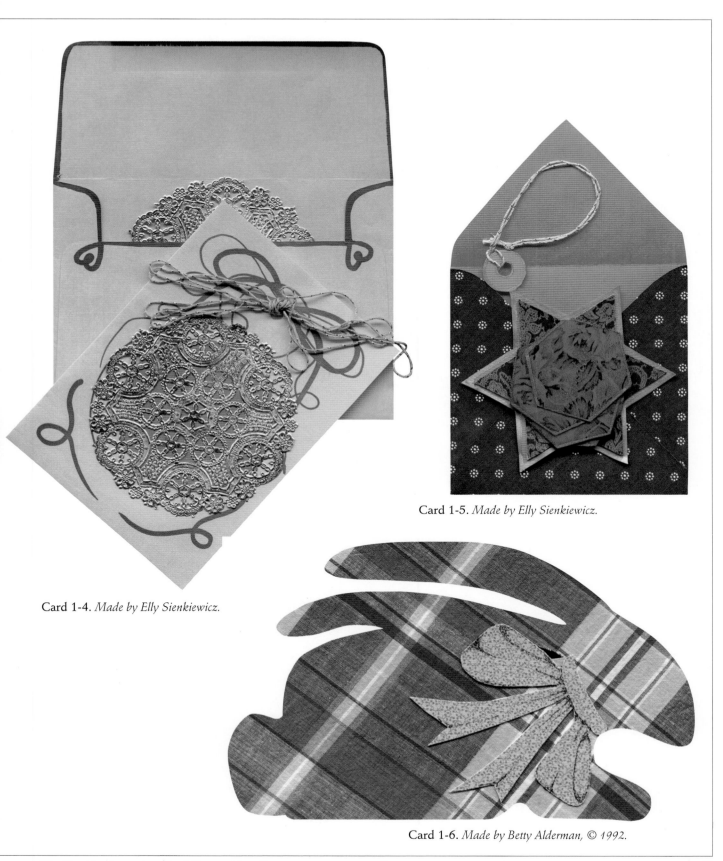

Card 1-4. *Made by Elly Sienkiewicz.*

Card 1-5. *Made by Elly Sienkiewicz.*

Card 1-6. *Made by Betty Alderman, © 1992.*

Bear Up!

Dear Mary,
Hope you're
feeling
better!
Love, Elly

Flat Cards: Perfect Postcards Ideal Invitations

- *Cards: Heart and Hand Postcard, Teddy Bear Birthday Invitation*
- *Techniques: Layering Appliqué, A Birthday Invitation: Child-tailoring the Card, Kid Appeal Memo, Ink Embellishment*
- *Editorial Element: Adding an Inscription, Line Texture, Creating Anticipation*
- *Gift Greeting: "My Hand" — a Matted and Framed Picture*
- *Special Materials: Standard red card stock, file cards*

How brief, how succinct, how appreciated is the postcard! The flat card is the simplest of all cards to design, make, and send. Postcards (originally called "Penny Post-cards") crossed the country before World War I and have been created, sent, and collected ever since. We'll start right in on this favorite form of paper communication and in the process, we'll learn more steps for making paper greetings. These basics are so simple, the applications to ever widening creativity so easy, that after a postcard or two, there will be no stopping you. The format is simple: a flat card of a hand holding a heart. Pick the occasion, choose the sentiment, and inscribe it with your message. When a group of us has tackled this heart and hand card assignment together in a class, the varieties we come up with are wondrous. Yours will be, too!

* ARTWORK RECIPE 4:

Make Cards with Multiple Appliqués

Heart and Hand Postcards

Preparation: To make Fig. 2-1, assemble two large white file cards and two sets of fused hearts and hands made from Template 8.

Layering: In appliqué, when two or more shapes overlap, one is placed first on the background, then the other is placed over it to some degree. This process is called layering. It is simply a matter of thinking the problem through. If we use Template 8 (Fig. 2-1), the sequence is simple. The hand is placed first and the smaller heart is positioned second, squarely inside (on top of) the palm. Then the fabric can be heat-bonded to the paper. (Please remember to iron the whole card surface, so that an isolated, ironed spot doesn't warp.)

But what if we want to have Template 8's larger heart held by the fingertips? What goes down first? Because the hand is the larger motif, position (but do not bond) it on the large white file card background. Tuck the heart over two fingertips and under one as in Fig. 2-1. Or have it float above, tied to the fingertips by a string (Template 9, Fig. 2-2). In both layering situations, the components are arranged first, then bonded second. Do this even when one piece goes smack on top of the other. Do it just on principle so that you see the whole picture before you set it for eternity!

Teddy Bear Birthday Invitation: I've Grown!

Now let's up the ante by having lots of appliqués, lots of layering. Because flat cards

mail easily without an envelope, they make great one-step invitations. Twenty years ago I made my son Alex invitations to a party for his third birthday. I wanted to tailor the card to a child, so I chose his favorite teddy bear motif. To make Template 10 of fused cloth shapes, which goes on top of which (Fig. 2-3, p. 48)? Again, lay the whole design out first, adjusting so that the Teddy fits the card nicely. Dab a glue stick behind each unit and paste them down to prevent shifting when you iron. Then bond the card with heat.

Layering Order: The bear's head shows above the collar of the shirt. It must be put down second. Positioning order is sometimes a matter of judgment, so the sequence in Fig. 2-3 is a suggestion. The template's dotted lines show overlapping seams and explains Fig. 2-3's logic. Layering fits better than abutting — putting one raw edge against another. In fused appliqué, only the edges lapped under need a seam. Those seams are drawn right on the templates themselves. Inscribe card, front and back (Fig. 2-3, p. 48, and Fig. 2-4, p. 49).

Writing an Invitation: This card's invitation is on the side without fabric. The tone of an invitation should be welcoming. Formally this is phrased, "The pleasure of your company is requested at...." Informal invitations can begin with a title announcing "An Invitation" or simply, "A Birthday Party" (or "Shower," etc.). It's nice to end this sort of declaratory invitation with a warm sign off such as "We hope you can come!" But if our flat cards are to mail without an envelope, we need to get both the address and the invitation on one side. The writing is on the wall. These invitations need to convey just the facts! Your guest needs this information to pin up on the refrigerator: What? Why? (if applicable) When? Where?

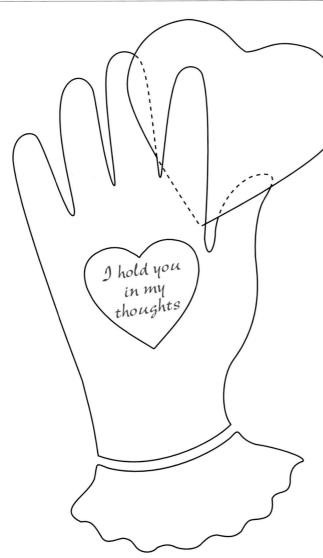

I hold you
in my
thoughts

Fig. 2-1. *Template 8. Artwork Recipe 4: Heart and Hand postcard made from a large file card.*

Thinking
of
you

And wishing you well

Fig. 2-2. *Template 9. Artwork Recipe 4: Heart and Hand postcard made on a small card.*

Fig. 2-3. *Template 10. Artwork Recipe 4: Teddy Bear
Birthday Invitation.*

Who is the host or hostess, and how to R.S.V.P.. Today, *respondez s'il vous plait* ("Please reply") increasingly reads, "R.S.V.P, Regrets only" and a phone number. Fig. 2-4 got all this on the card with enough extra room for a heartfelt "Please Come!"

Christmas Tree Postcard

Card Stock: Use a purchased, pre-stamped U.S. Postal Service postcard.

STANDARD POSTCARD

Onto regulation size postcard, bond a Christmas Tree made from Template 11, then inscribe it (Fig. 2-5).

Embellishment Option: What more could you do to embellish this card? You could take a fine, silver, felt-tip pen and dust the tree with sparkles. You could draw red hearts hanging off the branches, then shade the background behind the tree with tiny, black pen dots. My favorite way to shade with a pen is to cluster the dots more closely together the nearer they are to the fabric motif. See the background in Fig. 2-6, p.50, for example. Then have the dots dissipate and fade away from it. Let them turn

into a fine mist that eventually disappears. All this embellishment turns your postcard into a lovely card, one which will still mail at the lower postcard rate!

Speedup Spot: If you want to make lots of these cards, review the notes on mass production in Part 1. Choose a showy fabric since you'll want to leave off the embellishment to save time!

Fig. 2-5. *Template 11. Artwork Recipe 4: Easy, fast, and economical! This standard pre-stamped USPS postcard has a fused green Christmas tree already to be topped with a gummed gold star! With good scissors you can make hundreds of these, efficiently.*

Alex's Birthday Party

When: Tuesday, March 7th
 3:00 – 5:00 p.m.
Where: 5540 30th Street, N.W.
R.S.V.P.: Elly Sienkiewicz
 244-0781

Please Come!

Firstclass

To: Master Evan Bageris
 14 Chestnut Street
 Wellesley, MA
 02117

Fig. 2-4. *Artwork Recipe 4: Reverse side of Teddy Bear Birthday Invitation.*

OVERSIZE POSTCARD

Cut out a fused fabric Template 12 (Fig 2-6), Christmas Tree appliqué. Position it on a 4¼" x 11" flat, red card. (For quantity and good value, order a ream of 8½" x 11" red cover stock from your printer and have him cut it in half for you.) When the tree is bonded to a card of this size, there is room for a lengthy inscription. One year I wrote under the tree a thought remembered inexactly from a brass plaque on the Old Post Office Building in Washington, D.C.:

Old trees are like old friends,
They tie us to our past,
They give stability to our present,
They promise hope for the future.

Making and sending those cards was such a happy holiday visit with family and old friends. I didn't even mind that I had to pay first class letter postage for an odd-size postcard!

Fig. 2-6. *Template 12. Artwork Recipe 4: This 3½" x 5" card is the largest size mailable at the post card rate.*

Money-Saving Tip

A POSTCARD IN THE EYES OF THE U.S.P.S.

Oh my gosh! Our expanding government is even regulating greeting cards. I just got a card "Returned to Sender" by the U.S. Postal Service. Stamped in red was "Ten cents additional postage due. Non-standard size envelope." This followed the earlier shock of being told by the Post Office that this lesson's Christmas Tree Postcard was too big to mail at the lower postcard rate. For the 60 cards I'd made and addressed, it cost more than ten cents extra per card to mail them at the first class letter rate. By making flat cards no larger than 4¼" high x 6" long (and no smaller than 3½" high x 5" long) you can send them at the official U.S. Postal Service First Class Postcard Rate. Off-size or off-shape (they must be rectangular) pops them up to Letter Rate. Regrettably, it gets more complicated yet. Envelopes mail at first class rates if kept within these dimensions:

- Letter-Size Mail must be no larger than 6⅛" high x 11½" long (or no smaller than 3½" high x 5" long) and no more than ¼" thick.
- Flat-Size Mail (for those super size greetings!) must be no larger than 12" high x 15" long, or more than ¾" thick.
- Card or envelope attachments? These must "totally adhered to the card surface" and should not be "an encumbrance to postal processing." What is the good news? I studied a thick up-to-date postal code ring binder and found regulations — such as the one against square letter mail — that seem ignored or perhaps never absorbed by postal processors. In my own experience, even most of what I now realize must be off-size letters have mailed without a hitch. In sum I think our chances of sending whatever we make are excellent. Now that's a happy thought!
- And what about stamps? Do you remember sticking your postal stamp upside down in the upper right-hand corner? As youngsters, we were careful about when and for whom we did this because it means "I love you." Any letter which could bear S.W.A.K. on its flap, could surely also carry one of these head-over-heels stamps. Do today's children know this means Sealed With A Kiss? Perhaps not, for the Victorian language of stamps was barely known by the time of my own youth. My Victorian grandmother, on the other hand, knew just what a sideways stamp meant, one stamp in the upper left-hand corner, one on its side, and one facing up from the lower left-hand corner. This bit of our culture has slipped away from most Americans. Today, as far as I could tell, not even the postal regulations dictate how we must place our stamps!

Kid-Appeal Cards

Children of all ages enjoy making appliquéd paper greetings. Preschoolers can paste on sequins or lay out a crazy patchwork of fused scraps for you to iron. You may spot one of their drawings, a snowman perhaps, which can be translated into a fused appliqué. Hung dustily on a wall, I have a paper plate, filled with wet plaster at one time, where four-year-old Alex imprinted his hand. His teacher wrote such an endearing poem on the back of the plate that even though Alex is now 23, I may never be able to throw away! Hands are special. There are a variety of drawing styles. But no stylization is quite like tracing the hand of a loved one!

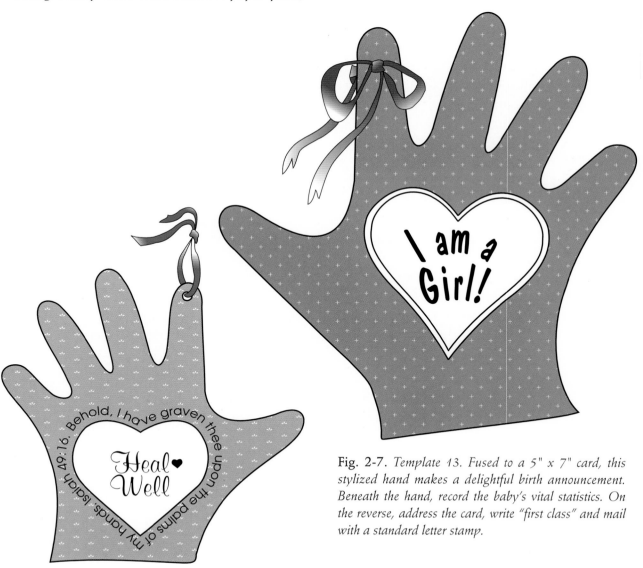

Fig. 2-7. *Template 13. Fused to a 5" x 7" card, this stylized hand makes a delightful birth announcement. Beneath the hand, record the baby's vital statistics. On the reverse, address the card, write "first class" and mail with a standard letter stamp.*

Fig. 2-8. *A hand cut-out can make a hanging "Thinking of You" card.*

Gift Greeting:
"My Hand" Matted Picture

Supplies:
- Strathmore Art Paper color coordinated to the project's fabric.
- Purchased picture mat: outside measurements 8" x 10", with 5" x 7" opening.

Parents and grandparents are softies for treasuring a memento of their wee one's fleeting childhood. The card, My Hand, is inspired by Alex's plaster of Paris hand print and the primary school teacher who helped him make it for me. Perhaps you can make this card for someone who will appreciate it just as much and keep it just as long!

- Trace a child's hand onto the protective paper of a 6" swatch of fusible.
- Iron this marked fusible to the wrong side of a pretty fabric, then cut out the fused hand appliqué.
- Cut an 8" wide x 10" high rectangle of art paper.
- Position the mat over the paper. With pencil, trace the shape of the mat's opening on the paper. For positioning, mark the opening's horizontal center with a piece of removable tape.
- Position the hand so that the wrist touches the top of the tape and is centered in the window from left to right. Remove the tape and bond the appliqué to the paper with heat.
- If the hand is an infant's, border it with a circle. Use a bold black or silver marker. Beneath it, with a fine, black, felt-tip pen, inscribe the following poem. Underneath it, write the child's full name, age, and the date.

This is my hand
So tiny and small
For you to hang
Upon the wall
So you can see
As the years go by
How we've grown big
My hand and I!

Cover the picture mat with cloth. Cut a 10½" x 12½" rectangle of fused fabric. Lift off its protective paper. Use this paper to keep from fusing the mat cloth to the ironing board in this next step.

- Position the picture mat over the protected ironing cardboard. Center fused fabric rectangle, right side up, over the picture mat. Put a temporary straight pin in each of the four outer corners to hold the position. Bond the fabric to the picture mat with heat (Fig. 2-9, p. 54).
- From the wrong side, trim out the center fabric to 1" beyond the mat opening all around (Fig. 2-10, p. 54). Next cut a diagonal line into each corner, dividing (bisecting) the corner fabric equally (Fig. 2-10, p. 54). Clip out a square at each corner if you need to reduce bulk (Fig. 2-11, p. 54). Any raw edges at the corner will be hidden under the frame.
- Run a line of glue stick over the back of the mat board, ½" in from the inside edge. Finger press the cloth to this, pushing it in, up, and over it. One side at a time, iron the excess outside edges over to the backside of the mat.

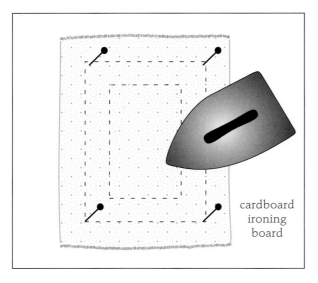

Fig. 2-9. *Position the picture mat over the protected cardboard. Center the fused fabric right side up over mat.*

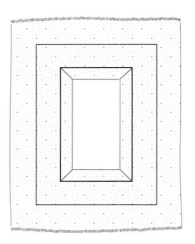

Fig. 2-10. *Cut the fused cloth out of the center, leaving 1" bordering the inside of the picture mat.*

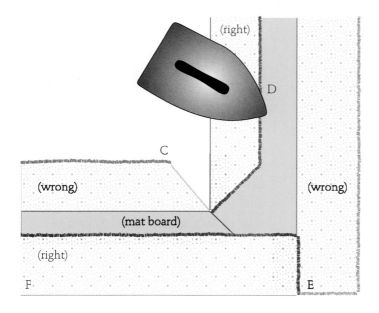

Fig. 2-11. *Clip out a square at each outside corner, if you need to reduce the bulk.*

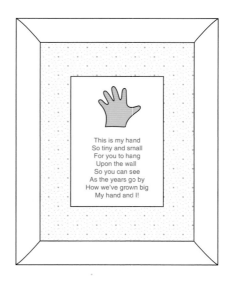

Fig. 2-12. *My Hand — a framed, cloth-matted picture inscribed with an endearing verse.*

• Position the finished mat over the hand/poem picture and slip it into a standard 8" x 10" opening frame (Fig. 2-12).

If you want to mail this, leave it without a frame and mail it in a cardboard reinforced photo mailer. Your photo shop has these. Cardboard priority letter mailers from the Post Office also work.

This small framed token hints at fantastic frameable art inspired by the flat card concept. In the color photos, Betty Alderman's birth announcement or primitive cat would make wonderful hung pictures! From the flat card's limitless possibilities, let's move on to explore the flat, folded card. Even something so familiar holds surprises for us in Lesson 3.

Card 2-1. *Made by Betty Alderman, © 1992.*

Card 2-2. *Made by Betty Alderman, © 1992.*

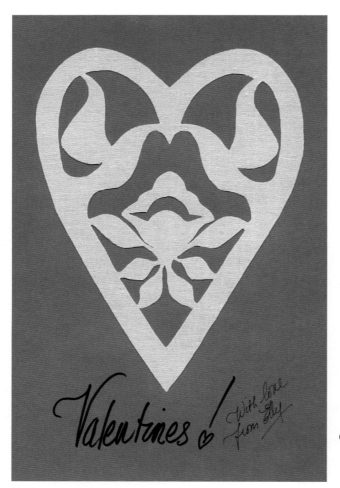

Card 2-3. *Made by Elly Sienkiewicz.*

Card 2-4. *Made by Betty Alderman, © 1992.*

Card 2-5. *Made by Betty Alderman.*

Card 2-6. *Made by Betty Alderman.*

Card 2-7. *Made by Irene Keating.*

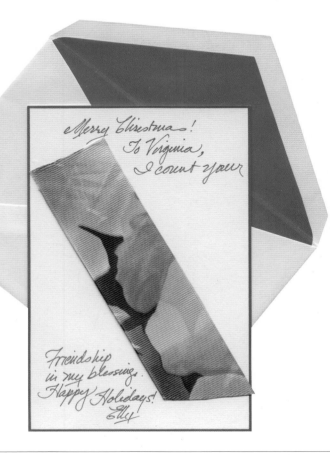

Card 2-8. *Made by Elly Sienkiewicz.*

Card 2-9, right. *Made by Elly Sienkiewicz.*

Mount the Cut-out Heart onto a Folded Card

- *Cards: A Token of Affection, a Plethora of Folded Cards*
- *Techniques: Scoring a Fold; Gluing, Slits, Raised Mountings; Going to the Edge: The Deckled Edge, The Pinked Edge, Double-Edged, the Cut-Out Edge, more on the Gilded Edge, and Interlocking Edges*
- *Editorial Element: "Plays" on the heart symbol: Seeking the Unexpected; Surprise, Make a Folded Card for Editorial Punch*
- *Gift Greetings: Family Photo Album Enclosure, Spill-outs, Hanging Ornament, or Booster Necklace Medallion*
- *Success Spot: Not for Children Only: Tuck in a Treat! Lagniappe! Surprise! Your Card Overfloweth*
- *Special Materials: Confetti shapes and other novelties*

Once the decorative motif is mounted on a folded card, an editorial element begun on the front of the card can continue inside. Mounting the heart motif gives more freedom to the artwork as well, since embellishments can be placed on the surrounding card surface. For ease, we'll refer to a folded card as though it were made up of pages. The cover is page 1; the back of the cover, page 2; the right-hand inside page is page 3; the back of page 3 is page 4. On a triptych (three panel card) the pages are numbered: cover, page 1; back of cover page 2; center page, page 3; right-hand page, page 4; back of right-hand page, page 5; back of center page, page 6.

Lesson 3

Beyond these basics are numerous other card folds. None has so impressed me as the pocket-sized family photo album which Cheryl Trostrud-White sent to me entitled "Merry Christmas Greetings from California, 1993" (Fig. 3-5). The pictures on this so clever gift greeting are photocopied snapshots and the album is made entirely from a hand-folded standard 8½" x 11" sheet of photocopy paper. With a mat knife, the paper is slit down the center from point a to point b, then folded into an eight-page booklet. Figs. 3-1 through 3-5 show you how to fold this delight and where the top of your snapshots must be placed on the photocopy master for the final product to read like a book. If you make this clever album enclosure for an appliquéd greeting, thank Cheryl!

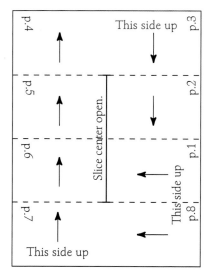

Fig. 3-1. *Diagram of album pages showing which side of the photo should be up.*

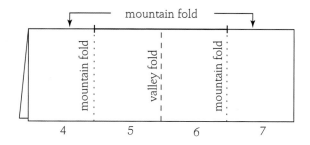

Fig. 3-2. *Diagram showing how to fold the sheet double on-the-fold, after slicing the center open with an art knife.*

Fig. 3-3. *Bird's eye view of folding the sheet to open as a book.*

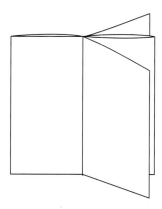

Fig. 3-4. *The folded album, open.*

Fig. 3-5. *The folded album, closed.*

* ARTWORK RECIPE 5:

Scoring Paper for a Clean Fold

The bigger the card, the heavier its paper-weight must be to support it. Size can be an important design element. The standard example is the oversized Valentine given to convey a largess of love. The heavier the paper, though, the more difficult it can be to fold, particularly if you have to fold it against the grain. (See Part 1.) Scoring, making an indentation in the paper, solves this. To fold a card closed, score the inside of the card.

- Use a stylus pen, the tip of a medium-fine metal crochet hook, or a butter knife to score paper.
- Mark with pencil the beginning and end points of the fold line (Fig. 3-6A).
- Position a steel-edged ruler to the left of, but touching, these points. With your left middle finger and your thumb extended, press down hard on the ruler to hold it steady (Fig. 3-6B).
- With your right hand, pull the butter knife toward you (guided against the ruler) while pressing down to make a shallow channel in the paper (Fig. 3-6C). Fold page 1 to the right, making its edge even with the right edge of page 3. Press the crease to sharpen the fold (Fig. 3-6D).

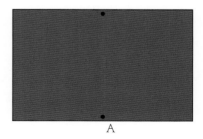

Fig. 3-6A. *Scoring cardstock for a clean fold.*

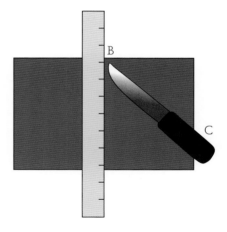

Fig. 3-6, B–C.

Fig. 3-6D.

* ARTWORK RECIPE 6:

Mountain Folds and Valley Folds

An easy terminology labels the upwards fold a "mountain fold," an inverted fold, a "valley fold" (Figs. 3-7, A–C). A mountain fold is marked on the patterns with a dotted line. (I remember this by thinking of the dot-like chocolate candy, telling myself "M and M's" is for a mountain fold.) To make this fold, score the back of the card. For a valley fold (marked with a dashed line) score the inside of the card.

WHERE TO FOLD A CARD

Most cards are folded down the middle so that the card opens up like a book. Figs. 3-8, A–C and 3-9, A–B, show some card folding options.
- One fold card:
    A. Center-folded in half horizontally
    B. Center-folded in half vertically
    C. Off-center folded vertically
- Two vertical valley folds makes a triptych card (Figs. 3-11, A–C, p. 64).
- If you alternate one vertical mountain fold with one vertical valley fold twice, it makes an accordion card (Figs. 3-10, A–B).

Fig. 3-7A. *Mountain fold.*

Fig. 3-8A. *Fold in half horizontally.*

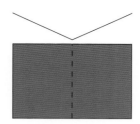

Fig. 3-7B. *Valley fold.*

Fig. 3-8B. *Fold in half vertically.*

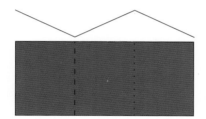

Fig. 3-7C. *Valley fold / mountain fold.*

Fig. 3-8C. *Fold off-center vertically.*

Fig. 3-9A. *Two vertical valley folds make a tryptich card.*

Fig. 3-9B. *Tryptich card.*

Fig. 3-10A & B (right and below). *The accordion card; valley, mountain, valley, and mountain fold. Let the accordion concept inspire the editorial element.*

page 1

page 2   page 3   page 4   page 5   page 6

Fig. 3-10, A–C. *Two vertical folds make a triptych card.*

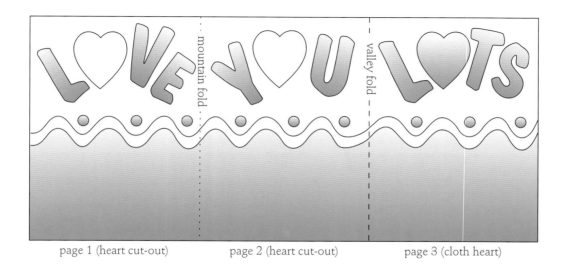

page 1 (heart cut-out)   page 2 (heart cut-out)   page 3 (cloth heart)

* ARTWORK RECIPE 7:

Make a Folded Card for a Surprise Editorial Element

CARD: A LOVE TOKEN

Years ago my mother sent me and each of my children such an endearing handmade card that I've kept mine ever since. It is so simple, personal, and versatile, that I'm delighted to share her card with you. It is a folded card and because folded cards set the viewer up on page 1 and then deliver the punch line on page 3, they often contain elements of humor and surprise. This one had both. On the front was a hand with simple daisy shapes floating around its fingertips. Airily written among the flowers was the timeless question, "How do I love you?" And the answer, "Let me count the ways..." Then inside, the unexpected exclamation, "OOPS! Not enough fingers!" The hand was my mother's, traced. Instantly recognizable, that hand made the card forever a keepsake. To make your own:

- Fold a 8½" x 11" sheet of art paper in half so that the card opens on the right (Fig. 3-7A, p. 62).
- Draw around your hand onto fusible protective paper backing. Cut a swatch of fusible, ½" bigger than the drawn hand, bond it to the chosen cloth's wrong side. Next, cut the hand out on the drawn line, making of it an iron-on cloth patch.
- Position the hand appliqué on the card's first page so that there is room for a bordered margin around it (Fig. 3-11). Bond the appliqué to the paper.
- In two bold felt-tip pen colors, write

"How do I love you? Let me count the ways..." across the hand. Decorate the white space with looped daisies, then write inside the card: "OOPS! Not enough fingers!"

Fig. 3-11. *Sample of page 1 and 3 of the Love Token card.*

Lesson 3

Kid-Appeal Tip

Children love surprises! If you tuck a card folded in half into an envelope, fold first, it can hold a surprise. You can fill the card's valley fold crease with a sprinkling of some surprise. (When the card is opened, you can be sure the contents will spill out on the table or on the recipient's lap. Surprise!) A Valentine's card might have a pretty heart appliqué on the outside, an inscription, "Lots of sweet wishes for Valentine's Day!" inside, and a cascade of cinnamon heart candy or flat candy hearts imprinted with messages. An orange heart appliqué on the card's outside might have a jack o'lantern face inked on it (Fig. A). The message inside, "Happy Halloween!," would have been preceded by black plastic ants falling into the recipient's lap! Card shops, gift shops, paper stores, and variety stores have a wealth of metallic or plastic confetti cutouts and other tokens to tuck into a child's card. Tumble-out surprises are not for children, only. When I wanted to send a fabulous invitation to my 50th birthday, I enclosed a silk rose, a scroll of quotations on friendship, and metallic confetti cut to read that year's date. (You have to purchase confetti with dates and years around or before New Year's day!) A tea bag, a stick of chewing gum, a baseball card, bubblegum pack, candy corn, shoelaces, stickers, a bumper sticker, or even postage stamps are items that can be tucked in which will surely inspire a clever card from you and a smile from the one who receives it!.

Boo! Love to you!

or

"Happy Halloween!"

Fig. A. *Halloween card.*

Not for Children Only

Fig. B shows a decorative Christmas ball (one fabric fused-to-card stock circle, glued on top of another circle ½" wider in diameter) tied to page 1 of a folded card. The method is simple: punch two holes in page 1 and one or two holes in the ornament. then tie the two together with gold string. This is a way to make a multitude of small decorative circles with inspirational messages. These medallions could hang from a window or lamp, or even as a pendant around the recipient's neck. "Smile. You're alive!" "Don't wait to hear a good song: Sing one!" "Ain't nothing' never so bad but that it couldn't be worse." "Catch a moment of wonder!" or "Gather ye rosebuds while ye may." Each of us could use a bit of positive thinking and encouragement. (To find it nestled in the morning's mail among the bills and advertising would be an unexpected delight!)

Is there more to folded cards? There is a lot more. "Stick with me, baby," said the Folded Card. "There's a whole world out there we haven't seen yet!" For starters, in the next lesson, the Folded Card shows you how versatile a card with a window can be. And that's still just a small window at that, on the wide, wonderful, world of cloth-on-paper card making.

Fig. B. *A removable Christmas tree ball is tied by gold cord to this card. Gold marker edges the ball and draws more bow on the card itself.*

*ARTWORK RECIPE 8:

Going to the Edge

Cards folded off center invite you to decorate the edge of the first page, or the third page, or both. We've already learned gilding as a decorative paper edge finish. More decorative edgings follow.

- Pinking shears come saw-toothed or scalloped. There is a a rotary cutter on the market that will cut scallops. There are also inexpensive paper scissors for children with a variety of decorative edges.
- Deckled Edge. With your left hand, press a steel-edged ruler down on the paper, leaving a 1" margin to the right. Firmly grasp the top of this margin with your right-hand and tear the 1" strip off, pulling the paper against the sharp straight edge and forward towards you (Fig. 3-12A).
- Pasted Ornamentation Edge. Paste a textured ornamental edge (ribbon, trim, fabric, or paper) behind, but peeking out from under the edge (Fig. 3-13).
- Shaped Edge. The edge can be cut into any shape you like. Edges with simple shapes are shown in Figs. 3-14, p. 70–71, 3-15, p.72, and 3-16, p. 73.
- More Gilding On-the-Edge. Beyond one-line gilding, consider setting up a pattern. Draw one fine line, leave ⅛" space, then add a bold line at the edge (Fig. 3-12A). Or perhaps draw a line of bold, gold dots just in front of the gilded edge (Fig. 3-16, p. 73).

Fig. 3-12A. *Dove card with off-set deckle edges and a lined border. Slit to hold a real ribbon.*

A
Friend

Is a present
you give yourself.

Thank you
for being mine!

And may time bring you peace.

Fig. 3-12B. *Dove card page 3.*

Fig. 3-13. *Ribbon lightly glued to the gift box is echoed by a ribbon glued to the edge of page 1. The streamer folded to the back hangs free.*

Fig. 3-14A. *Page 1 with a simple shaped corner.*

Appliqué Paper Greetings – Elly Sienkiewicz

Fig. 3-14B. *Page 3 repeats the same simple shaped corner.*

Fig. 3-15A. *Page 1 shows a shaped edge, cut to let page 3 show.*

Please help us celebrate!

Fig. 3-15B. *Page 2.*

Happy Birthday!

Fig. 3-16. *The shaped edge of page 1 repeats the shape of the cake.*

Lesson 3

Seeking the Unexpected: Plays on a Heart's Meaning

A "play" on a symbol takes its meaning lightly, uses that symbol adroitly in an unexpected way. Plays on a heart symbol are well-loved and instantly recognized. Use this formula: Picture the heart, functioning as something other than a heart, on the front of the card. Already you are suggesting something special and off-beat about this heart. Write the punch line inside the card on page 3. For example:

This gift carries fond wishes!

My heart lifts at thoughts of you! **or** *Wherever I am, I miss you!*

When you're happy

I feel glad,

When you feel bad,

I'm so sad.

Get Well Soon.

74

Appliqué Paper Greetings — Elly Sienkiewicz

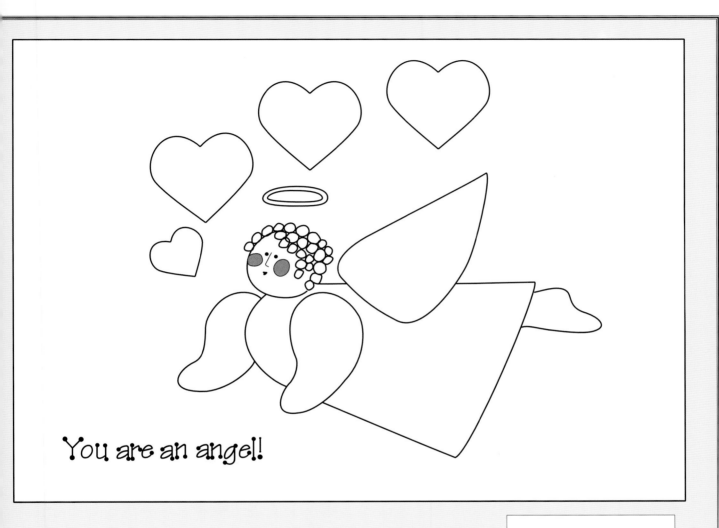

You are an angel!

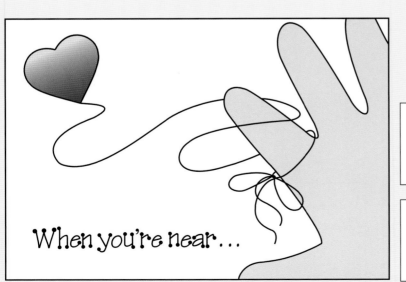

When you're near...

Thank you for your thoughtfulness

My heart soars!

or

Safe Journeying!

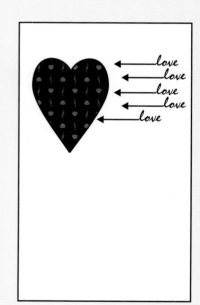

My heart
is
yours!

I LOVE YOU!

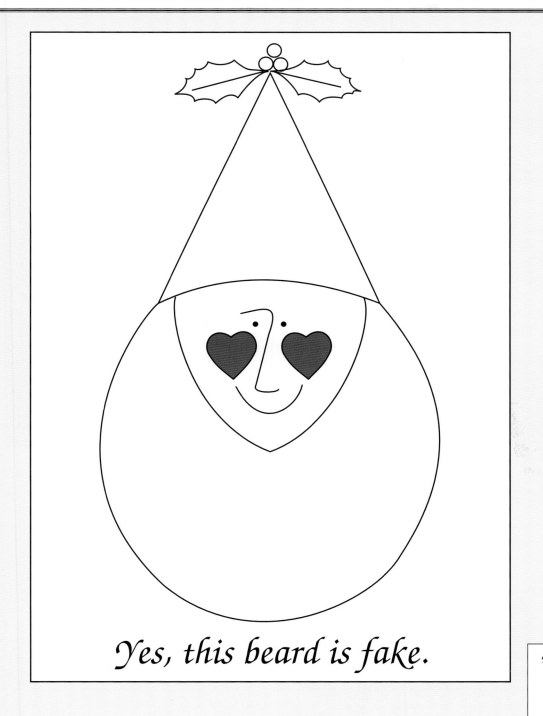

Yes, this beard is fake.

But our fond thoughts
of you are real.

Merry Christmas
and
Happy New Year

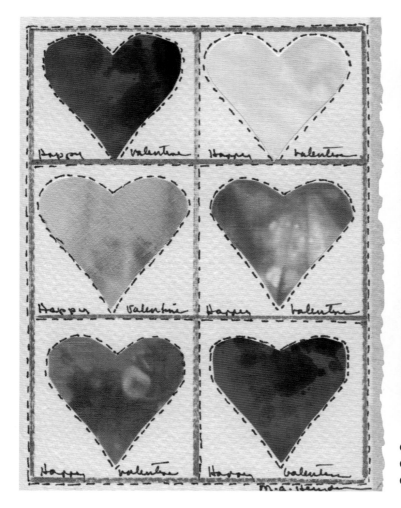

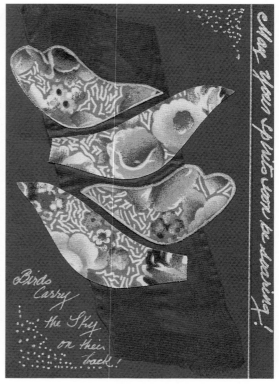

Card 3-1, left. *Made by Mary Ann Herndon.*
Card 3-2, above. *Made by Elly Sienkiewicz.*
Card 3-3, below. *Made by Elly Sienkiewicz.*

Card 3-4. *Made by Elly Sienkiewicz.*

Card 3-5. *Made by Elly Sienkiewicz.*

Card 3-6, left. *Made by Elly Sienkiewicz.*

Card Windows to Frame a Conversation Print, Photo, Fancy Ribbon, Collage, or an Inscription

- *Cards: You've Stolen My Heart; "This is My Heart Without You."*
  Collage Cards, Friendship Cards, Interlocked Hearts, Clasped Hands
- *Technique: Silhouette Shapes, Windows Open or Shuttered, Collage,*
  Clasped Edges
- *Editorial Element: Surprise*
- *Special Material: Foam core or styrofoam mounts; found objects to*
  weave into cards

Cut a hole on page 1, the outside of the card. You will have fashioned a picture frame, a window on the inside world of the card. Your window adds a bit of mystery to the card, a hint that what meets the eye is not all that there is. The window can be an open porthole. The window can have a shade or awning to be lifted up from bottom to top. Or it can be shuttered on the left and on the right, inviting the recipient to part the shutters. For added mystery, the shutters that are page 1 and page 5 can have cut-out edges which interlock. Suspense mounts as they are opened gingerly to reveal the surprise inside!

Fig. 4-1. *Heart-shaped window card.*

Each day I hold you in
my heart and
love you more and more.

or

Wishing you
a beautiful bloom!

There are two good places to put the card's inside design:

- Paste the secondary decoration to the back of page 1 which is page 2. The heart-shaped window in Fig. 4-1, for example, reveals a slightly larger heart pasted behind it on page 2. That heart is decorated with dimensional, ribbon-trimmed petunias from a later lesson.

Alternatively:

- Position the secondary decoration inside on page 3. If done this way, the cut-out shape on page 1 remains an open porthole window. By contrast, Fig. 4-2's window (an envelope) is shuttered with a flap to be lifted open. In the envelope card, the element framed by the window is an inscription written on page 1. Experiment! However you use a window's promise — both physical and symbolical — it will add to your card-making pleasure.

Card: You've Stolen My Heart

- Fold a 7" x 8" rectangle of card stock in half vertically to begin the card pictured in Fig. 4-3, p. 84.
- With a fine-tip, black marker, grid the outside of the card into twelve 2" squares and frame this unit with a ½" border.
- Using Template 13, Fig. 4-3, p. 84, cut 12 fused heart appliqués.
- Open the card out flat. Bond 11 of these hearts, one each to a drawn square on page 1. (Set each heart in place with a dab of glue from a glue stick, before ironing the whole card to bond them to it.). But in the second row down from the top, the second square in, simply draw the heart, cut the card stock out on this line, and remove it. Also slit open the sides and bottom of this square and score a valley fold across its top so that this flap lifts like a window shade. Beneath this missing heart write "you've stolen my heart!"

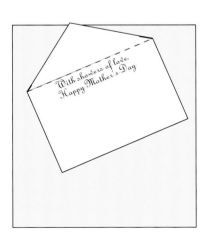

Fig. 4-2. *Envelope window lifts to deliver the message.*

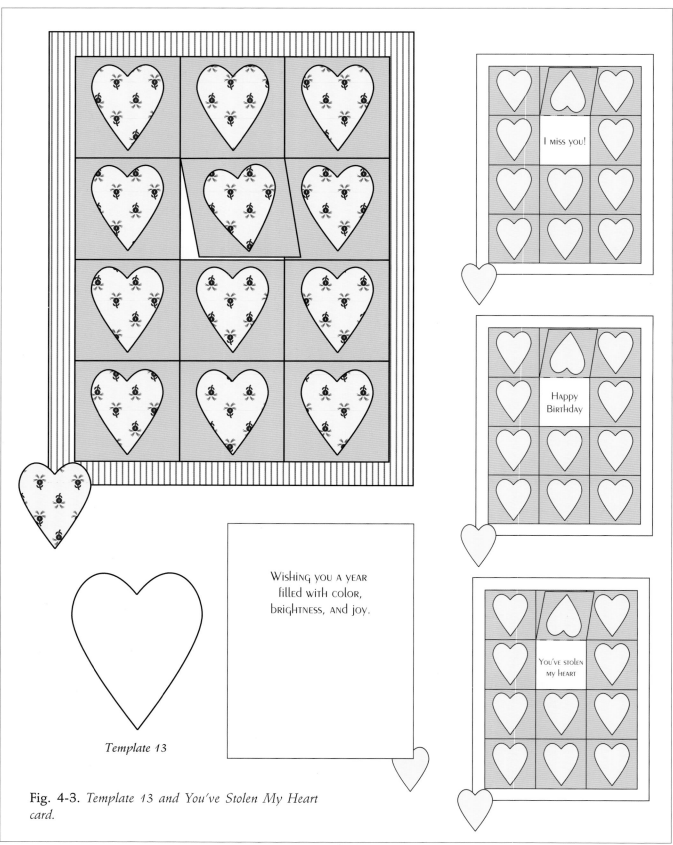

Template 13

Wishing you a year filled with color, brightness, and joy.

I miss you!

Happy Birthday

You've stolen my heart

Fig. 4-3. *Template 13 and You've Stolen My Heart card.*

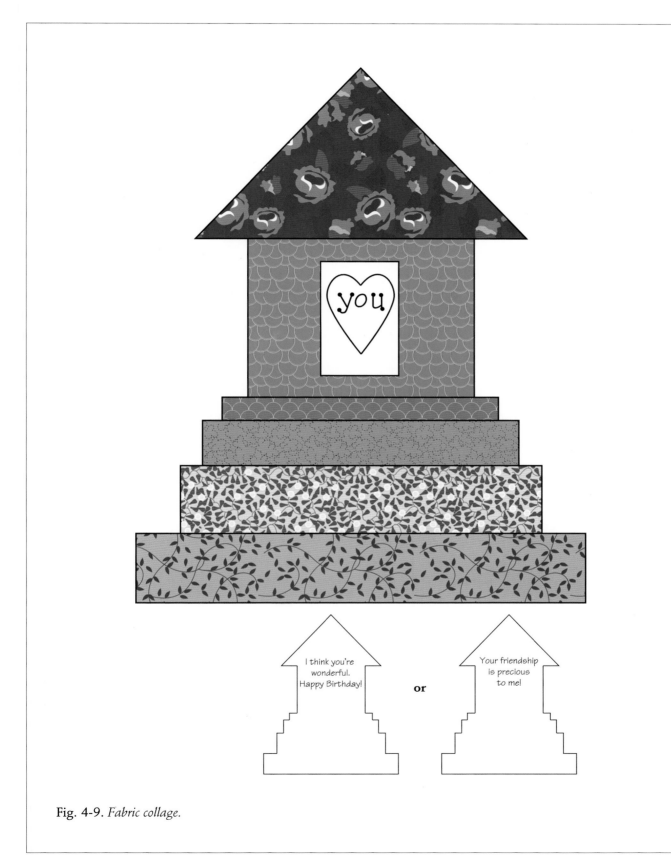

Fig. 4-9. *Fabric collage.*

Fig. 4-10. *Hearts in a collage.*

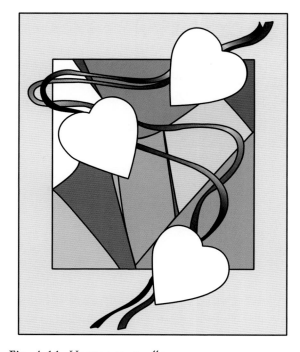

Fig. 4-11. *Hearts over a collage.*

* ARTWORK RECIPE 11:

Fancy Shutters, Interlocking Hearts, Clasped Hands & Other Overlapping Edges

A three-paneled card with pages 1 and 5 opening to reveal page 3 is a simple concept. One assumes a clean-cut rectangle cut into three equal parts folded right over center, then left over center. This works! But we, like our Victorian foremothers, can get more complex and much fancier. Consider:

- The card in Fig. 4-12 folds horizontally into three parts and is sealed with a heart on page 1. When the card is shut, the point of the heart slips into a slit in page 5 and forms a clasp.
- The edges of the card (a 5" x 13" rectangle) in Fig. 4-13, p. 92, interlock. Page 1 is 3" x 5" and page 5 is 2" x 5". The right-side margins of the top holly leaf and the bottom heart are slit enough for page 5 to slip beneath them. The page 5 card stock is cut vertically but also around the tip of the holly leaf. When page 5 is slipped under the slits of page 1's holly leaf and heart, the card stays closed.
- Likewise, in Fig. 4-14, p. 92, the top heart on page 1 can be slit around so that page 5 can slip under it to hold the card closed. A slit inside this card allows another heart to be lifted out, and its message read.
- In Fig. 4-15's, p. 93, Clasped Hearts card, a 7" x 11" rectangle has been folded so that page 1 is 3½" wide

including the protruding bottom heart cut-out. Page 3 is 5" x 7" and page 5 is 2½" wide, including the protruding top heart cut-out. The hearts interlock when the card is closed.

- Fig. 4-16, p. 94, is based on a vintage Victorian enclosure card. Working on the outside of the card, fuse a heart and printed posies, construct a man's hand and a woman's out of cloth, positioned as shown. Use good Bristol paper for this, and score the valley folds (marked on the outside as mountain folds) from the inside of the card. When closed, the woman's hand links into the man's, and all on a bed of posies! The reproduction of a Victorian original printed by John Grossman inspired this interpretation. Figs. 4-17A–C, p. 94–95, show envelope designs to fit the Clasped Hands Card.

Not only are these Lesson 4 techniques endless with possibilities, but the folded card's versatility is still unraveling. In the next lesson we'll use the folded card's sturdiness to support a wealth of dimension. Even as we make these appliquéd paper greetings, dimensional cards are enjoying a renaissance unprecedented since the mass-produced greeting card originated a century and a half ago!

>slits

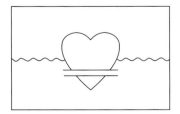

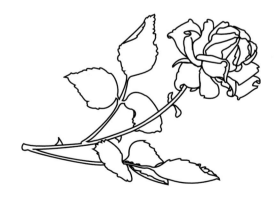

Fig. 4-12. *Card open full size (top), closed (left), and "posie" for the inside of card. Inside card, above flower: "Accept this posie from a friend," below flower, "Whose love for you will never end."*

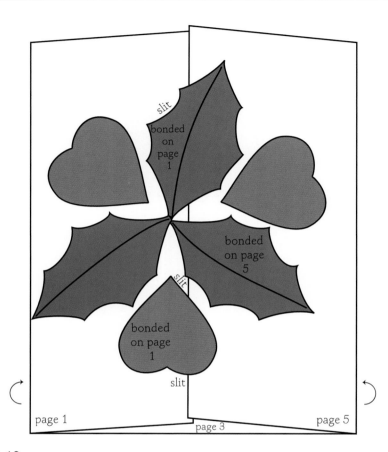

slit

bonded
on page
1

bonded
on page
5

slit

bonded
on page
1

slit

page 1

page 3

page 5

Fig. 4-13.

*All hearts return home.
Our love is with you
this Christmas Season.*

Fig. 4-14.

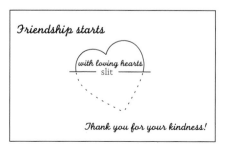

Friendship starts

with loving hearts
slit

Thank you for your kindness!

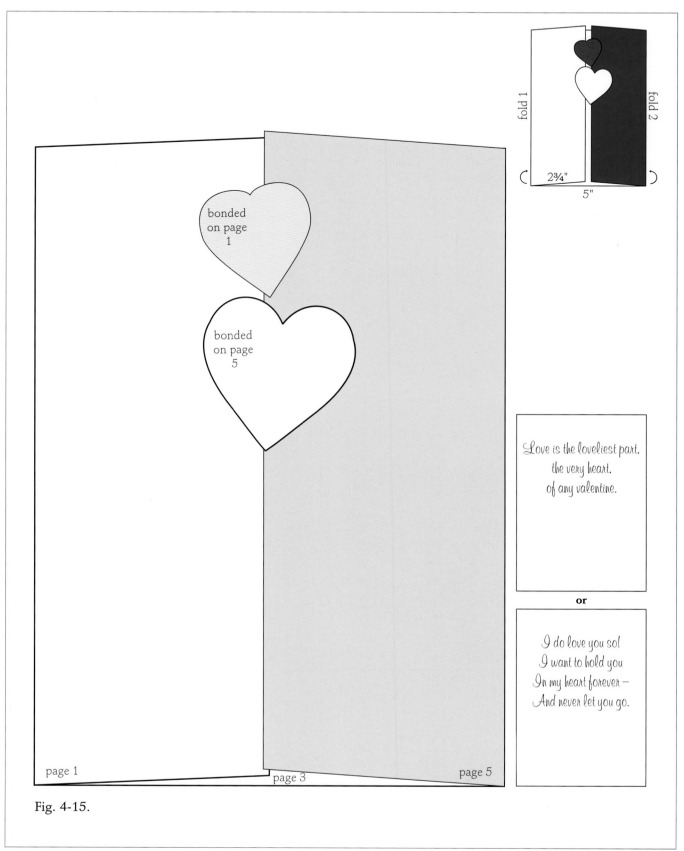

fold 1

fold 2

2¾"

5"

bonded
on page
1

bonded
on page
5

Love is the loveliest part.
the very heart.
of any valentine.

or

I do love you so!
I want to hold you
In my heart forever —
And never let you go.

page 1

page 3

page 5

Fig. 4-15.

Fig. 4-16. *Clasped hands card pattern.*

Fig. 4-17A. *Closed envelope: Version I of Fig. 17B.*

Appliqué Paper Greetings — Elly Sienkiewicz

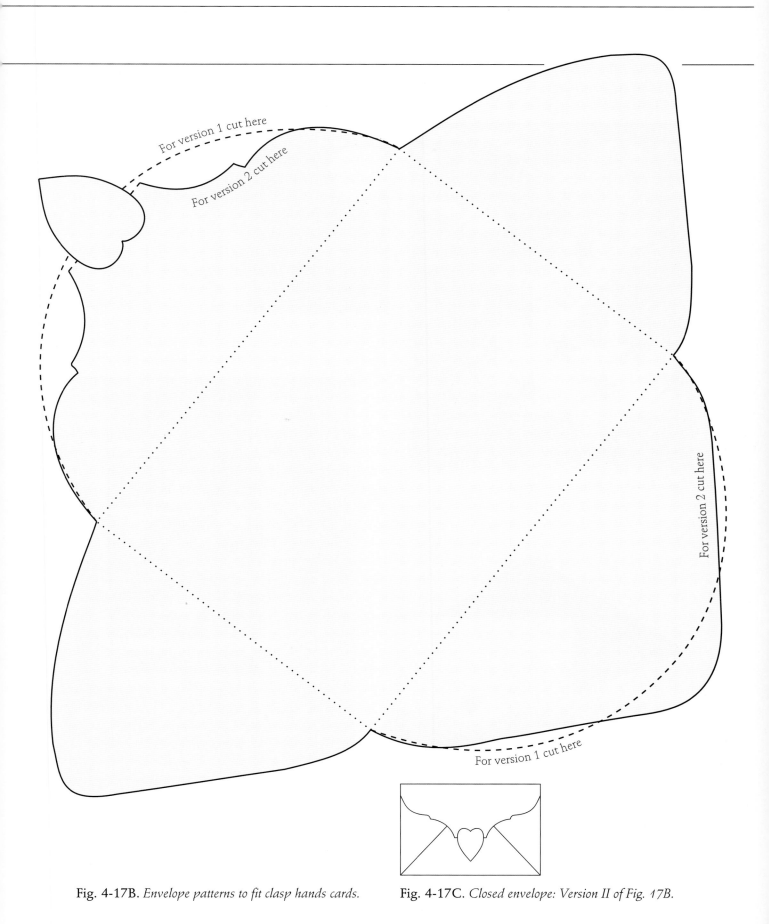

For version 1 cut here

For version 2 cut here

For version 2 cut here

For version 1 cut here

Fig. 4-17B. *Envelope patterns to fit clasp hands cards.*

Fig. 4-17C. *Closed envelope: Version II of Fig. 17B.*

Card 4-1. *Made by Betty Alderman, © 1992.*

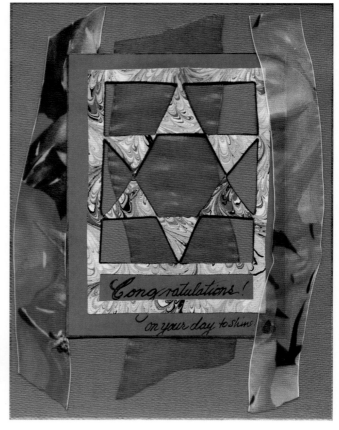

Card 4-2. *Made by Elly Sienkiewicz.*

Card 4-3, left. *Made by Elly Sienkiewicz.*

Card 4-4. *Made by Faye Labanaris.*

Card 4-5. *Made by Elly Sienkiewicz.*

We hope this helps give wings to your Dream

With our love to you

* ARTWORK RECIPE 13:

Slits: Bottomless Pockets

Slits are made with an art knife, using a steel or heavy Plexiglas ruler. Always work with the card open to one layer over a cardboard or self-sealing cutting mat. One slit or two are the most common and you see examples of this in Figs. 5-5, 5-6, and 5-7, p. 106.

I SEND YOU

HUGS

slit A

slit A

Fig. 5-5. *Teddy Bear slit card.*

Appliqué Paper Greetings – Elly Sienkiewicz

Slit open here. ↓

Cut double on the fold.

You are the
Heart of My Heart

Fig. 5-6. *Teddy Bear slit card.*

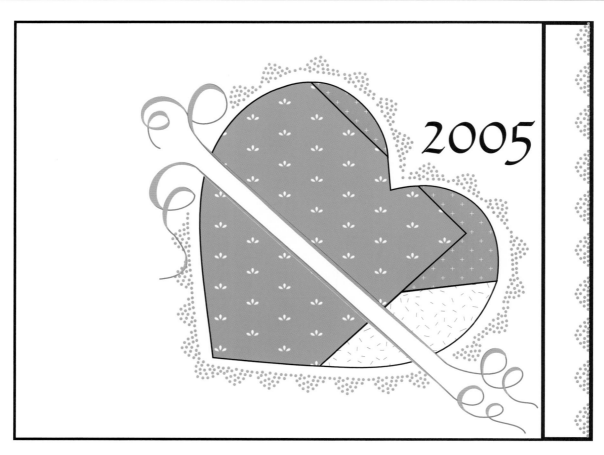

Fig. 5-7. *Template 15 (for the stuffed heart card).*

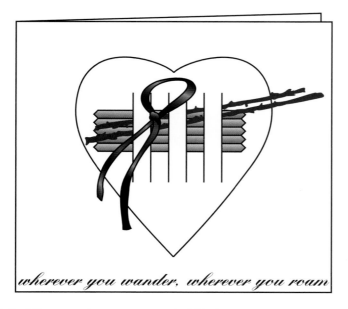

wherever you wander, wherever you roam

Be healthy and happy
and glad to come home.

Bon Voyage!

Fig. 5-8. *Slit paper heart woven with folded paper,
twigs, and ribbon.*

Weavability — One of Paper's Wonders, Too!

An ancient technology, paper is prominent in many of the world's folk arts. Paper folding makes us think of Japan and paper cutting turns our thoughts to Denmark, Germany, Mexico, China, and the Pennsylvania Dutch. On the other hand, paper weaving brings Scandinavia to mind. Fig. 5-10, p. 108, pays homage to both the Scandinavian woven heart and to a Pennsylvania German woven paper love token of a century ago. Slit paper is flexible. A set of parallel slits makes a band by which to attach a shell (or other small object) to a card (see Fig. 5-9). Perhaps a sophisticated montage appeals to you? Fig. 5-8 shows a restrained, almost Oriental presentation of a slit paper heart woven with an accordion fold paper, twigs, and a ribbon. On a larger scale this could be wall art!

Card: A Stuffed, Puffed Heart

- Fold an 8½" x 11" rectangle of rose-colored art paper into fourths. Hold it like a book. The "spine" is the fold on the left, the second fold tops the pages.
- Cut a fused fabric heart appliqué from the Template 15 heart pictured in Fig. 5-7. From thin quilt batting, cut a heart ¼" smaller all around than Template 15.
- With pencil, draw Template 15 on page 1 of the card.
- With a glue stick, lay a line of glue around the heart just inside the pencil line.
- Put another dab of glue in the center of the drawn heart and stick the batting heart on top of it. The batting sits inside the glue-drawn heart.
- Position the fused heart appliqué just a fraction inside the drawn heart to allow it to puff. Press it in place onto the glue. Then bond with heat the appliqué's edges by ironing to about a ⅓" depth.
- With a metallic marker, cover the heart's pencil line and decorate the outline of the heart beyond the fabric. For a finishing touch, scent the heart with cologne.

Card: Puffed Heart on the Inside

Card 4-4 (p. 97) by Faye Labanaris, shows a card containing a stuffed heart necklace. To make another version draw the Template 15 heart on page 1 and another one on page 3. Cut the page 1 heart out to make a window. Behind it, on page 3, make the puffed heart as in steps previous, starting with the second step. If this seems to beg for an editorial allusion, here are a couple of starts: "My heart swells with pride for you. Congratulations!" Or "My heart is filled with love for you!"

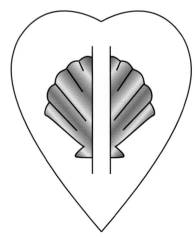

Fig. 5-9. *Card with shell in the slit. Inside: She'll be right!*

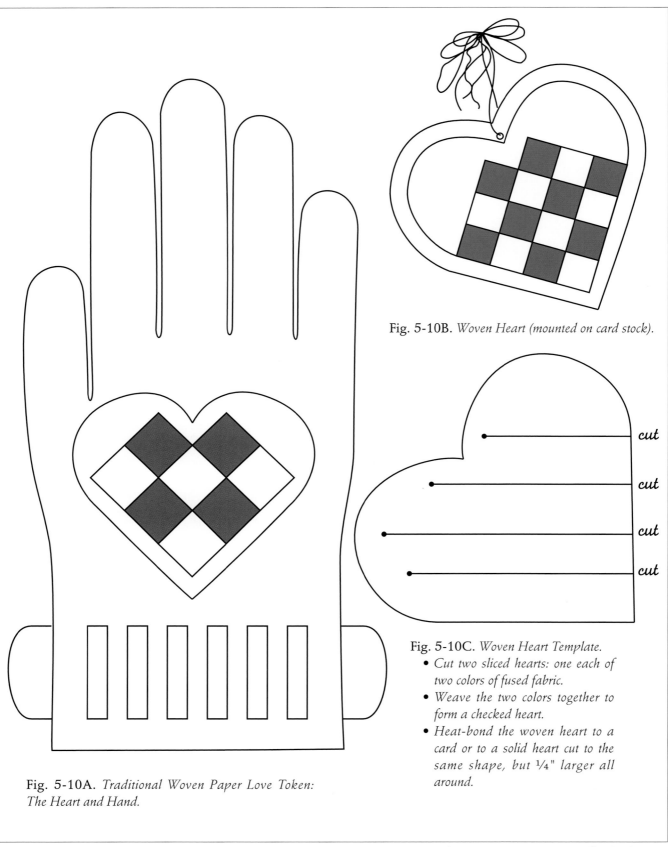

Fig. 5-10B. *Woven Heart (mounted on card stock).*

cut

cut

cut

cut

Fig. 5-10C. *Woven Heart Template.*
- *Cut two sliced hearts: one each of two colors of fused fabric.*
- *Weave the two colors together to form a checked heart.*
- *Heat-bond the woven heart to a card or to a solid heart cut to the same shape, but ¼" larger all around.*

Fig. 5-10A. *Traditional Woven Paper Love Token: The Heart and Hand.*

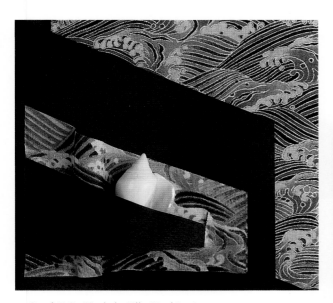

Card 5-3. *Made by Elly Sienkiewicz.*

Card 5-4. *Made by Elly Sienkiewicz.*

Card 5-5, left. *Made by Elly Sienkiewicz.*

Stand-up Cards, Pop-up Cards, Fancier Folds & Clever Cut-outs

- *Cards: Stand-Up and Pop-Up Christmas Tree Cards, Hollow Easter Egg Card, Linked Pop-Up Hearts, Sitting Dove, Stand-Up Hearts, Pop-Out Heart, Heart in a Heart, Pastorale Valley Pop-Up Card, Pop-Up Vase of Hearts and Flowers Card.*
- *Techniques: Tabs, Kick-Stands, and other ways to stand a card up; Cut-outs and Folding for Pop-Ups*

From whence comes our love for the stand-up card? I remember that a stand-up paper doll was something very special, as though that physical characteristic made her a bit more human and fun to be around. A shaped card which stands up, or some parts of it stand up, intrigues us. We appreciate the complexity. There is something about this turn-of-the-century time we live in which respects complexity. We are a bit mistrustful of quick fixes and simple answers. Where modern in the 60s meant sleek and simple, we accept more complexity all around us, no less in greeting cards. Beyond simple stand-ups are pop-up cards in which sections move forward, or pop up, when the card is opened. These cards abound today. There are not only a plethora of Victorian reproductions but also clever modern creations by paper engineers, designers of contemporary cards. Despite modern technology, the paper engineers use simple techniques, many of which we've already learned. These include gluing, mountain and valley folds, slits, and tabs and other similar pieces which hook into a slot. Fig. 6-1, p. 116, shows some simple paper engineering for making cards that stand up. Let's learn some simple methods by making these cards before moving on to do pop-ups.

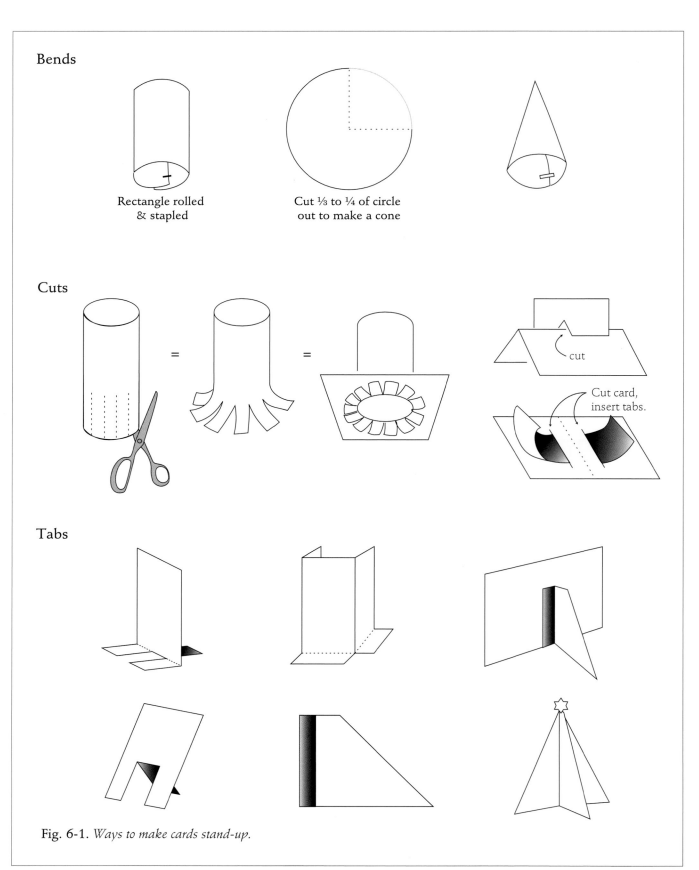

Bends

Rectangle rolled
& stapled

Cut ⅓ to ¼ of circle
out to make a cone

Cuts

=

=

cut

Cut card,
insert tabs.

Tabs

Fig. 6-1. *Ways to make cards stand-up.*

* ARTWORK RECIPE 16:

Cut First, Fold Second — Stand Up Cards from a Single Sheet of Paper

Card: Stand-Up Evergreen Tree

- To make the card pictured in Fig. 6-2, p. 118, cut a fused appliqué tree with Template 16.
- With pencil and ruler, lightly draw the horizontal center of a 3½" x 5" rectangle of red card stock. Draw it on the outside and on the inside of the card.
- Position the tree appliqué so that its horizontal center lines up with the midpoint you've just drawn on the cover of the card.
- Bond the tree to the card with heat.
- With an art knife, cut a slit outlining the tree above the card's midpoint line only.
- Turn the card over so that you are now working on the inside of it. Score a valley fold along the horizontal center, from one edge to the tree and from the other edge to the tree (not through the tree itself). Fold on the score line and look at the front of the card. The tree top will stand up (Fig. 6-3, p. 118)! This is the simplest kind of stand-up card to make.

* ARTWORK RECIPE 17:

Splicing Two Intersecting Shapes to Make a 3-D Stand Up Card

The simple, triangular Christmas Tree in Fig. 6-4, p. 119, the Christmas Tree Ball in Fig. 6-5, p. 119, and the dove in Fig. 6-6, p. 120, are all examples of cards where the cloth which gives the card color is fused first to both sides of the two intersecting shapes. Directions are noted next to each figure. When instructed to slit these shapes so they can be spliced together, use a sharp art knife on a protective mat. The slice must cut cleanly through two layers of cloth and one of card stock. Both cards will stand better if a stick-on seal or clear tape is used to hold them steadily together at the bottom and top.

*ARTWORK RECIPE 18:

Taking Single-Sheet "Cut First, Fold Second" Further!

Card: A Pop-Up Tree Card from a Single Sheet of Paper

Fig. 6-7, p. 121, shows a pop-up tree card so simple that you'll need no further instruction other than to remember that dots mean a mountain fold and dashes mean a valley fold! Doesn't this tree card look like fun to decorate?

Template 16

Fig. 6-2. *Stand-up tree card mails flat.*

Fig. 6-3. *Stand-up tree card folded.*

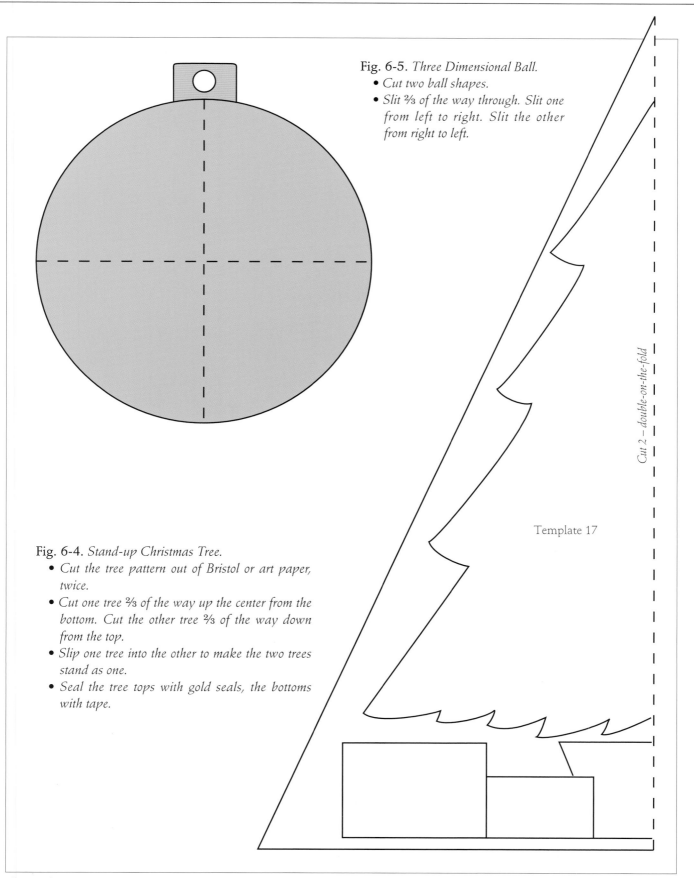

Fig. 6-5. *Three Dimensional Ball.*
- *Cut two ball shapes.*
- *Slit ⅔ of the way through. Slit one from left to right. Slit the other from right to left.*

Template 17

Cut 2 – double-on-the-fold

Fig. 6-4. *Stand-up Christmas Tree.*
- *Cut the tree pattern out of Bristol or art paper, twice.*
- *Cut one tree ⅔ of the way up the center from the bottom. Cut the other tree ⅔ of the way down from the top.*
- *Slip one tree into the other to make the two trees stand as one.*
- *Seal the tree tops with gold seals, the bottoms with tape.*

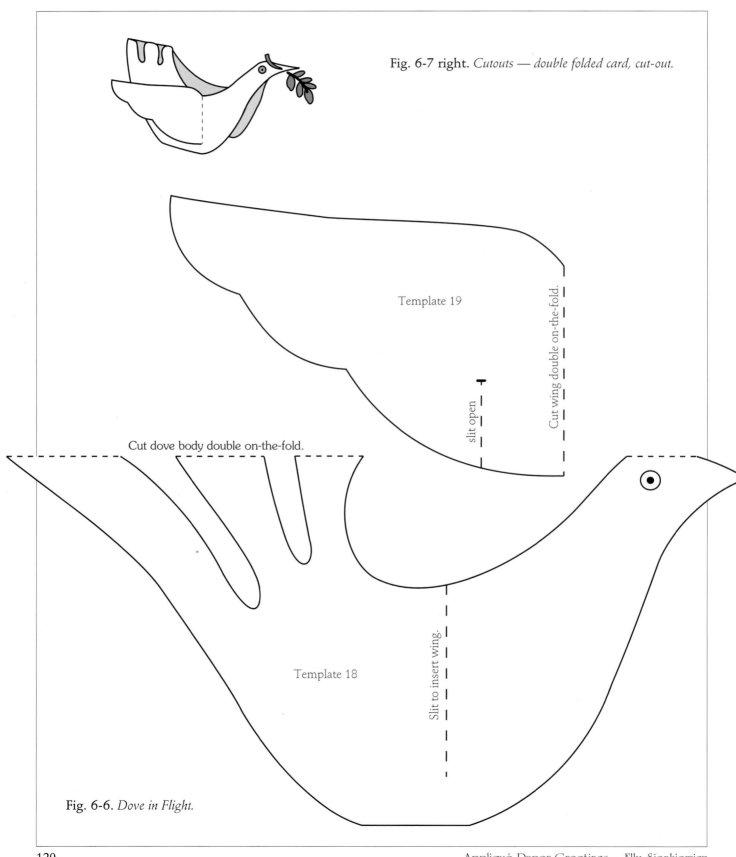

Fig. 6-7 right. *Cutouts — double folded card, cut-out.*

Template 19

Cut wing double on-the-fold.

slit open

Cut dove body double on-the-fold.

Slit to insert wing.

Template 18

Fig. 6-6. *Dove in Flight.*

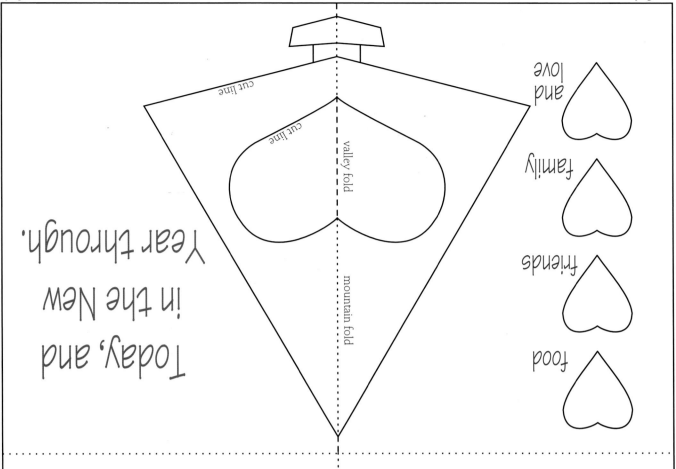

cut line

cut line

valley fold

mountain fold

love
and

family

friends

food

Today, and
in the New
Year through.

mountain fold

May All the
Good Gifts of
this Day ♡
Be Yours –

Card: Fancy Stand-Up Heart Card from a Single Sheet of Paper

- Cut one fused heart appliqué each with Templates 20 and 22. Cut two fused hearts with Template 21. Their placement is shown in Figs. 6-8A–C.

- With pencil and ruler lightly draw the horizontal center of a 3¾" x 7¾" rectangle of red cardstock. Draw it on the outside and on the inside of the card.

- Position the Template 22 heart on the inside of the card on page 3, so that its point A and B line up with the horizontal center. With heat, bond this heart to the card.

- Draw Template 22's cutting line C (above A and B). Still on the inside of the card, cut the open space out with an art knife (Fig 6-8C).

- From the inside of the card, score to make a valley fold at the card's center, to the right and left of the heart. Don't score where the heart has been fused on the inside of the card.

- When you fold the card closed, the bonded heart stands up. Bond the next (Template 21) heart appliqué onto page 2.

- Position the remaining fused cloth hearts as shown in Fig. 6-8D. Bond with heat.

Editorial Element: Lots of love. Or, I'm head over heels in love with you! Or, I'm falling, falling, falling in love, again. Happy Anniversary!

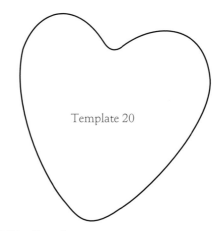

Fig. 6-8A. *Template 20.*

Fig. 6-8B. *Template 21.*

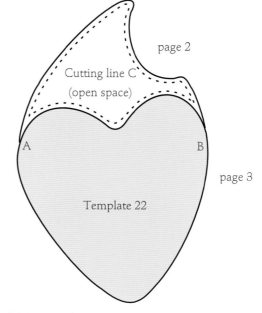

Fig. 6-8C. *Template 22.*

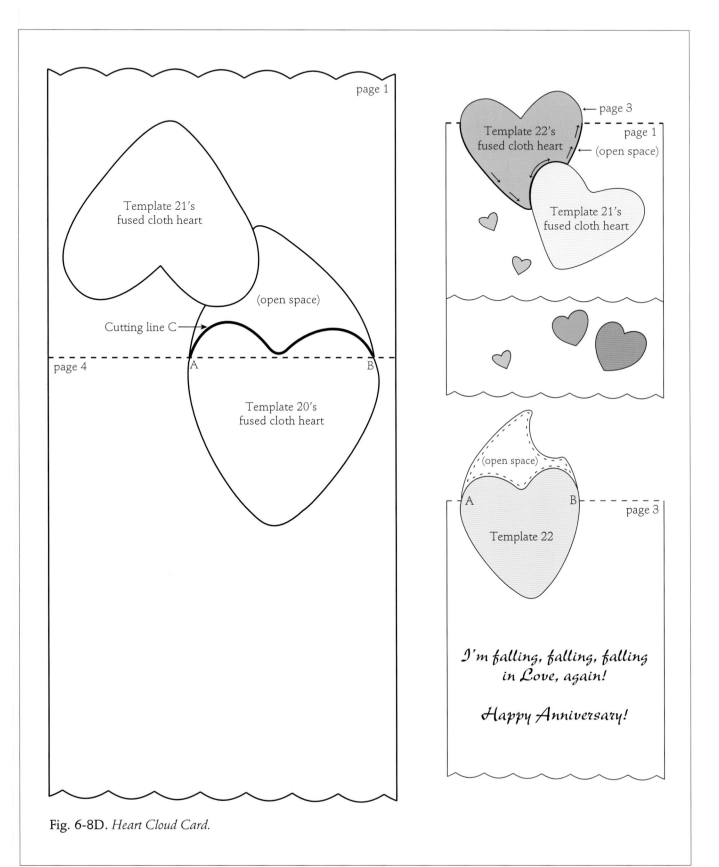

Template 21's
fused cloth heart

(open space)

Cutting line C →

page 4 ⌐ ─ ─ ─ A ────────────── B

Template 20's
fused cloth heart

page 1

→ page 3

Template 22's
fused cloth heart

→ (open space)

Template 21's
fused cloth heart

page 1

(open space)

A ─ ─ ─ ─ ─ B

Template 22

page 3

*I'm falling, falling, falling
in Love, again!*

Happy Anniversary!

Fig. 6-8D. *Heart Cloud Card.*

Fig. 6-9A. *Pop-up Heart Card.*
- Tab glued to back of page 2 so that it does not show on page 1.
- Slot marked and cut. Tab slipped through glued to back of page 3 so that it does not show on page 4.

Fig. 6-9B. *Template 23. Pop-up Heart Card.*

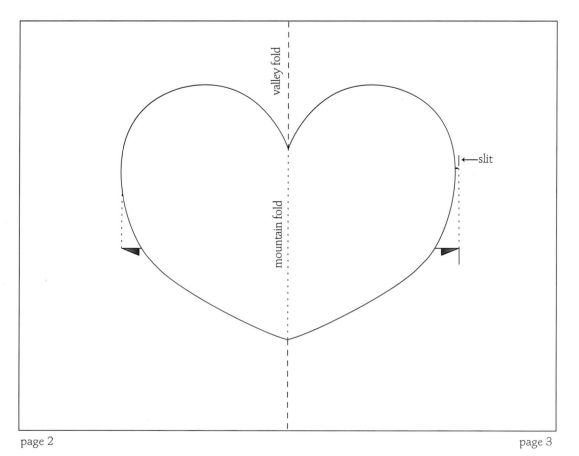

Pop-up Cards

* ARTWORK RECIPE 19:

Glued Tabs for Pop-up Dimension

Among the easiest pop-up constructions are tabs on the pop-up motif which pass through a slit in page 2 and 3, then fold to the back where they are secured by glue. The easiest way to hide these tabs is to fold a card in fourths like that in Fig. 6-7, p. 121, so that there is a front and a back to every page. The back of page 2 is hidden by the back of page 1 and vice versa.

Proud Pop-Up Heart Card

- Fold an 8½" x 11" card stock sheet into quarters.
- Inscribe page 1 as shown in Fig. 6-9A. Or decorate it with printed flowers cut out and heat bonded to the card.
- Heat bond Template 23's cloth heart to a card stock cut-out which includes both the Template 23 heart and its tabs.
- Inscribe the cloth heart.
- Slit pages 2 and 3 so that when the heart tabs are inserted the heart will move forward when the card is open.
- Thread the tabs through and glue them to the back side of pages 2 and 3.

For This is the Day Which the Lord Hath Made!

How complicated can a tabbed pop-up card get? Very! Fig. 6-10, p. 126 shows a card which sets a stage with a foreground, middle ground, and background. Its tabs are two different lengths: they have to be long enough to form a rectangle whose base is glued to the pop-up motif (the trees for example), to the card's stage, and to its background. The card diagrammed in Fig. 6-10A folds flat to fit in the envelope, then opens to a delightful dimension. The templates are to size. Once you understand the basic tab construction of these more complex cards, you'll find a challenge in replicating some of the Victorian prototypes, which reproduced abound in contemporary card shops!

Fig. 6-10A. *Scenic Pop-up Card.*
Stage set on page 2: Hills and mountains held by 5 fold tabs.

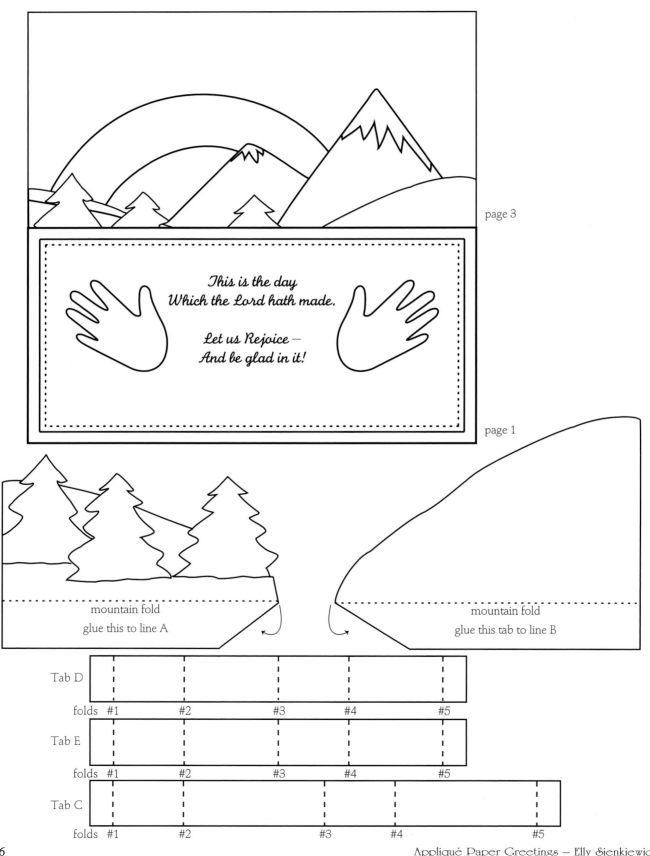

page 3

This is the day
Which the Lord hath made.

Let us Rejoice —
And be glad in it!

page 1

mountain fold
glue this to line A

mountain fold
glue this tab to line B

Tab D

folds #1 #2 #3 #4 #5

Tab E

folds #1 #2 #3 #4 #5

Tab C

folds #1 #2 #3 #4 #5

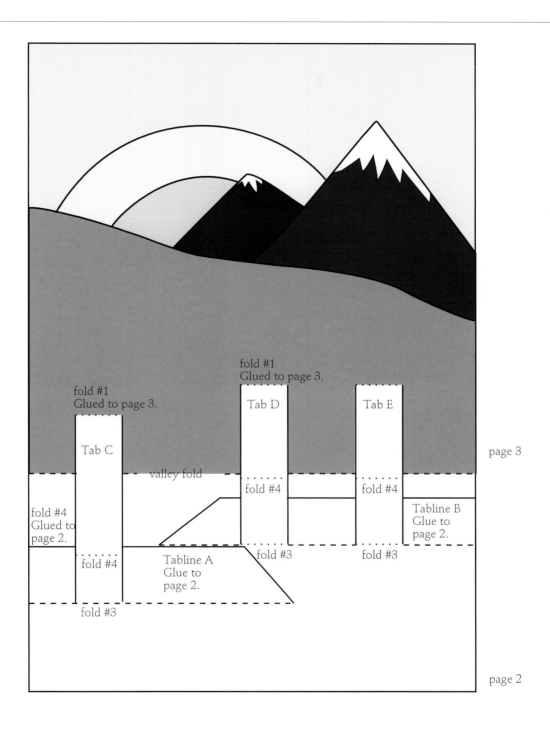

fold #1
Glued to page 3.

fold #1
Glued to page 3.

Tab C

Tab D

Tab E

page 3

valley fold

fold #4

fold #4

fold #4
Glued to
page 2.

Tabline B
Glue to
page 2.

fold #4

fold #3

fold #3

Tabline A
Glue to
page 2.

fold #3

page 2

Fig. 6-10B left. *Scenic Pop-up Card — Assembly patterns and tabs.*

Fig. 6-10C above. *Scenic Pop-up Card — Assembly tab placement.*

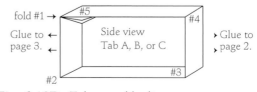

fold #1 →

Glue to ←
page 3. ←

#5

Side view
Tab A, B, or C

#4

#2

#3

▸ Glue to
▸ page 2.

Fig. 6-10D. *Tab assembly diagram.*

Hearts in a Vase

- To make the simple pop-up card pictured in Fig. 6-11B and G, begin with a 7" x 10" sheet of white Bristol board.
- On what will become the inside of the card, mark pencil dots at the center of the top and bottom edges of the card. Score the vertical line connecting these dots to make a valley fold (Fig. 6-11A).
- For the vase: Using Template 24, Fig. 6-11H, cut a 3" x 3¾" rectangle from a fused print. Center it with its base ¾" above the bottom edge of the card. Bond it with heat to the white card stock.
- With an art knife slit the card stock along the 3" base of the vase and again along its 3" brim (Fig. 6-11C).
- Close the card (Fig. 6-11D) and push the folded vase rectangle to the right (Fig. 6-11E). Crease it sharply.
- Lay the card flat so that pages 4 and 1 face upward. Score the center of the vase so that it makes a mountain fold on pages 2 and 3. From the inside, score the sides of the vase into valley folds.
- Use Templates 25 through 30, Fig. 6-11H to heat bond the leaf, heart, and flower shapes to card stock.
- Cut the hearts, leaves, and flowers out of the card stock and glue them inside the brim of the vase facing the recipient. Make sure they are not glued across the vase's center mountain fold.
- Now place a cloth cut-out of Template 31, Fig. 6-11J, p. 130, to the front of the card, page 1. Position it

so that it conceals the slits which allow the vase to pop forward. Glue the outer ½" margin of the heart only to page 1, being careful not to impede the movement of the vase.

Editorial Element: Outside, Flowers to you!; inside, Hope you're soon... in full bloom again! Or outside: When you're happy..., and inside, I blossom! Or outside, We enjoyed our visit with you so much; and inside, You give so much, so well! Or outside, I'm sorry, and inside, Please accept my apologies. Or, outside, We're so happy for you; and inside, Congratulations!

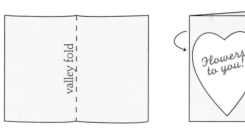

Fig. 6-11A.   Fig. 6-11B.

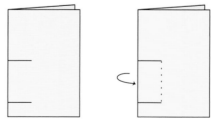

Fig. 6-11C.   Fig. 6-11D.

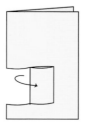
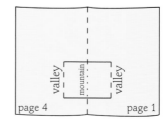

Fig. 6-11E.   Fig. 6-11F.

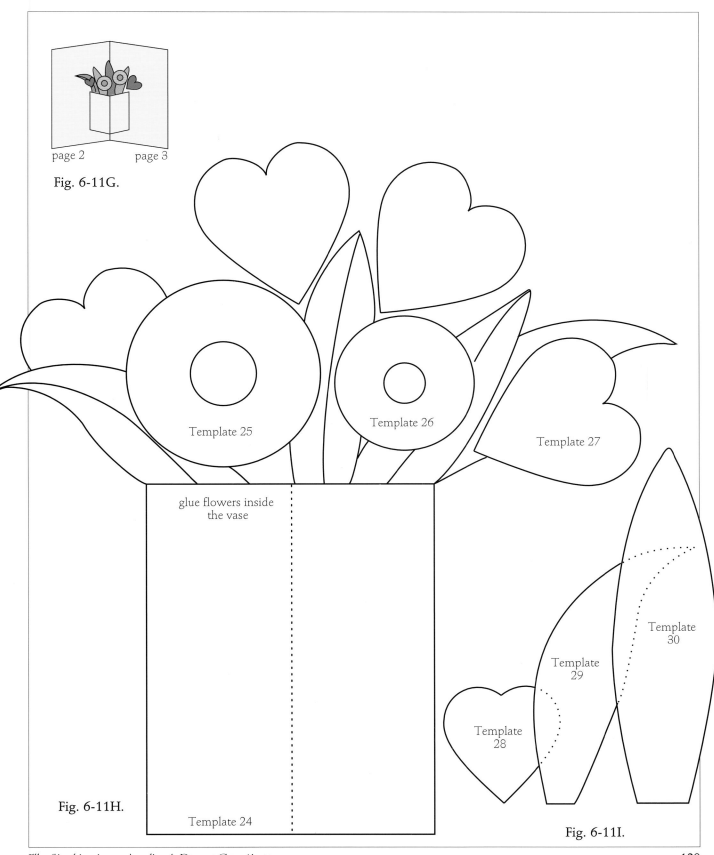

page 2   page 3

Fig. 6-11G.

Template 25

Template 26

Template 27

glue flowers inside
the vase

Template
30

Template
29

Template
28

Fig. 6-11H.

Template 24

Fig. 6-11I.

Get

Well

Soon

Template 31

page 1

Fig. 6-11J. *Heart: paste a plump heart to page 1 to cover the cut-out. Remember to glue the heart around its edges only. Inscribe page 1: "Flowers to You!" or "Get Well Soon."*

Appliqué Paper Greetings — Elly Sienkiewicz

Card: Hearts Linked in Love

- Fold a rectangle of white card stock, 9" x 13¼" into quarters (Fig. 6-12A).

- On the front, bond a posie of cut-out flowers. Tuck in a heart inscribed "With Love."

- Using the same floral print as in Step 2, ornament two heart-wreaths — one drawn onto white card stock (but not yet cut out) with Template 33, p. 133, and one drawn with Template 32, p. 133. Bond the flower cut-outs to decorate the heart wreaths.

- Next cut these card stock heart wreaths out around the flower shapes, allowing the edges to be a bit irregular as the print dictates. Make an irregular cut through the heart wreath as shown (Fig. 6-12F, p.133) 1½" up and to the right from the bottom point of the Template 32 wreath.

- Inside the card, on page 2 and 3, cut two 1¼" long slits as shown in Fig. 6-12B, p. 132. The slits begin 1¾" down from the horizontal fold. They are also equidistant from the vertical fold — 1¼" away at the top of the slit, ⁵⁄₁₆" away from the fold at the bottom of the slit.

- Insert the Template 33, p. 133, heart-wreath right-side up into these slits on page 2 and 3. Put rubber cement on the still exposed tab, as noted in Fig. 6-12B, p. 132.

- Slip the Template 32, p. 133, heart-wreath over the right-hand side of the Template 33, p. 133, wreath. Dab a bit of rubber cement on the underside of the slit. After a minute for the glue to set, press it firmly to the Template 32 tab.

- Cut a 1" x 1¾" card stock message card (Fig. 6-12E, p. 132). Inscribe it Thinking of You. Get Well soon. Happy Birthday. Be my Valentine. Thank you, Dear Friend. Then dab rubber cement on the message card's upper left corner and slip it into the page 3 slot, underneath the heart-wreath tabs (Fig. 6-12B, p. 132).

- Open the card all the way, and from the back, glue the tabs down, above the page 2 and 3 slits (Fig. 6-12C, p. 132).

- Returning to the inside of the finished card (Fig. 6-12D, p. 132), sign off "and more love!"

Envelope Information: The card fits in a 4¾" x 6⅞" envelope.

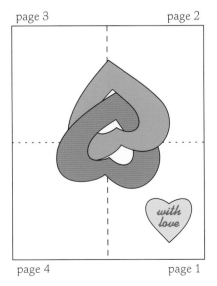

Fig. 6-12A. *Hearts Linked in Love Card.*

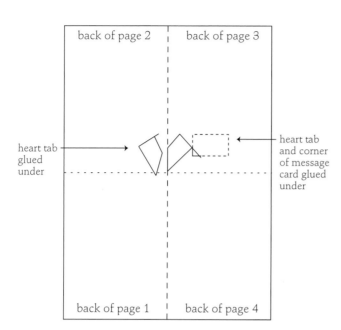

back of page 2 | back of page 3

heart tab glued under →

← heart tab and corner of message card glued under

back of page 1 | back of page 4

Fig. 6-12B. *Inside back of card.*

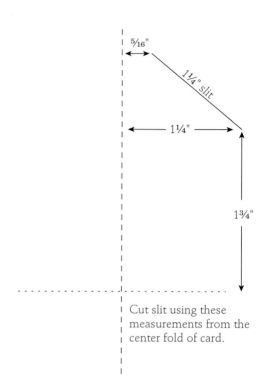

⁵⁄₁₆"

1¼" slit

1¼"

1¾"

Cut slit using these measurements from the center fold of card.

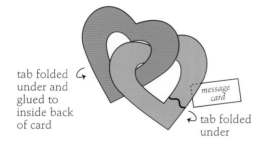

tab folded under and glued to inside back of card

message card

↳ tab folded under

Fig. 6-12C. *Hearts and message card, pages 2 and 3.*

Everything about you makes me love you so!

with love

page 1

Fig. 6-12D. *Card, page 1.*

I want to hold you close forever — and never let you go.

Fig. 6-12E. *Page 3.*

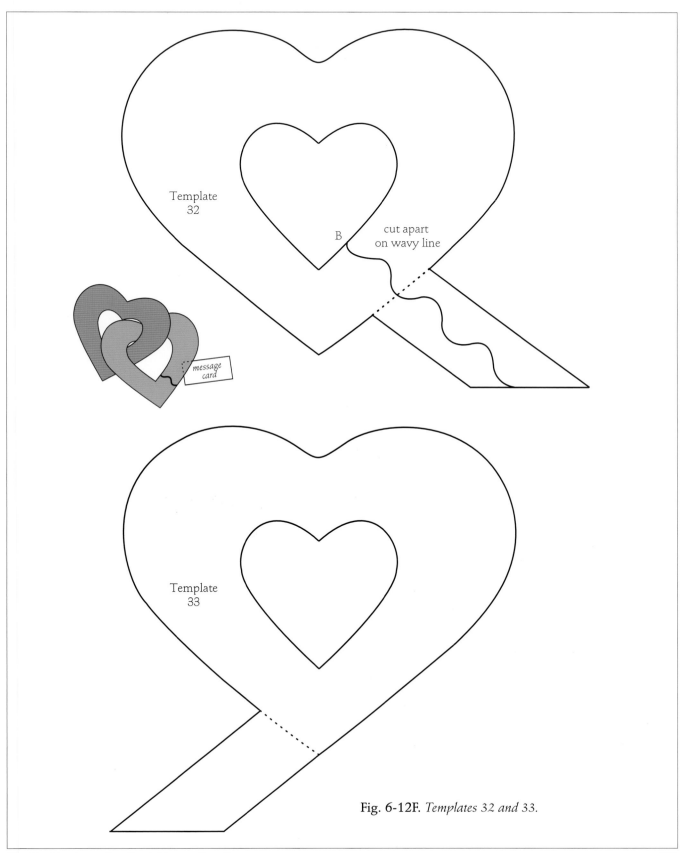

Template
32

B   cut apart
on wavy line

message
card

Template
33

Fig. 6-12F. *Templates 32 and 33.*

Card: Hollow Easter Egg with Hummingbird

The card pictured in Fig. 6-13B is more a stand-up card than a pop-up card. Done in a delicate floral print it is simply a lovely Easter card whose greatest challenge is to cut a wee hummingbird out of fused cloth! Below, in Plate 6-1, is an Easter Basket card by Betty Alderman. Why not try your own Easter design? Then on to Lesson 7 for simpler cards embellished by sewing machine and a posie of easy-to-make ribbon flowers for cards.

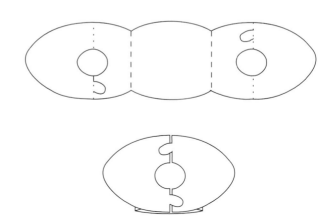

Fig. 6-13A. *Easter Egg fold-out card.*

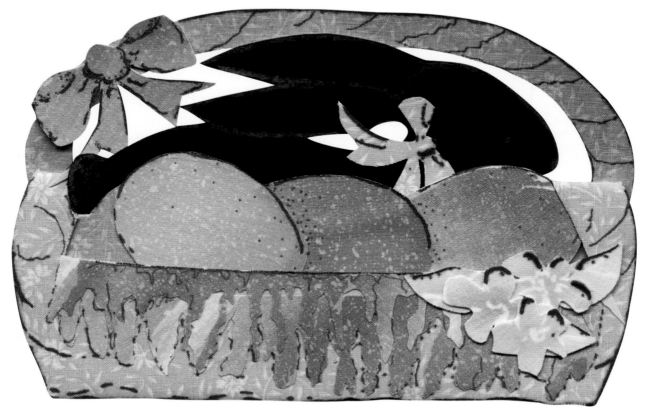

Card 6-1. *Easter Basket made by Betty Alderman, © 1992.*

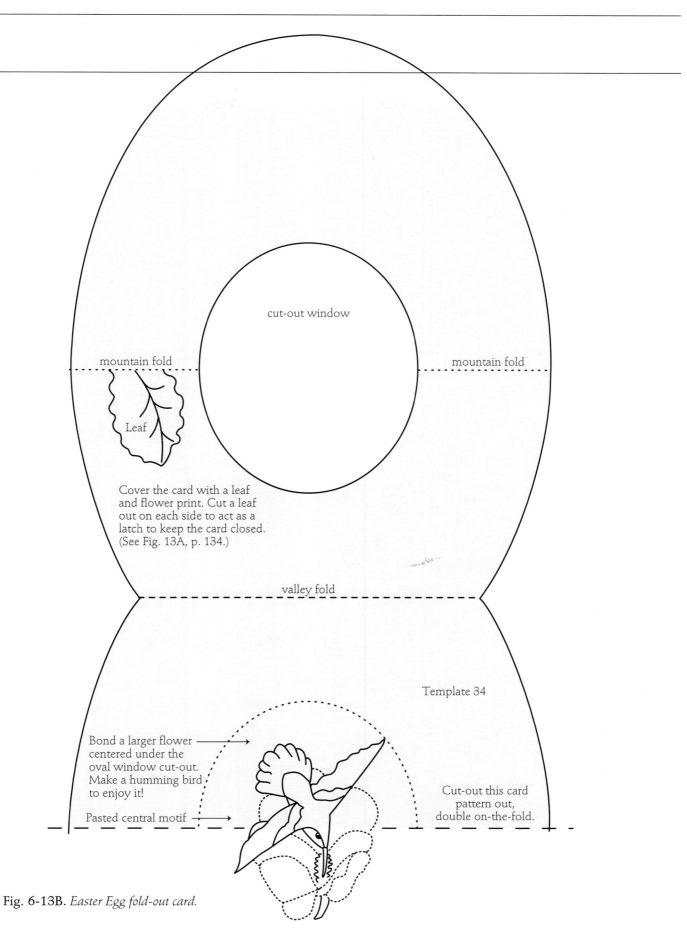

cut-out window

mountain fold   mountain fold

Leaf

Cover the card with a leaf
and flower print. Cut a leaf
out on each side to act as a
latch to keep the card closed.
(See Fig. 13A, p. 134.)

valley fold

Template 34

Bond a larger flower
centered under the
oval window cut-out.
Make a humming bird
to enjoy it!

Cut-out this card
pattern out,
double on-the-fold.

Pasted central motif

Fig. 6-13B. *Easter Egg fold-out card.*

Cards 6-2 through 6-6. *Decorative boxes made by Betty Alderman © 1992. Cards made by Elly Sienkiewicz, Betty Alderman, © 1992, and Kathie Campbell.*

Card 6-8. *Made by Betty Alderman, © 1992.*

Card 6-7. *Made by Elly Sienkiewicz.*

Card 6-9. *Made by Betty Alderman, © 1992.*

Card 6-10, below. *Made by Betty Alderman, © 1992.*

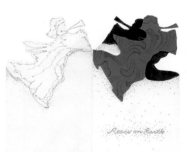

Appliqué Paper Greetings – Elly Sienkiewicz

Techno-fancies Sewing-machine Appliquéd Greetings & More Surprises

- *Cards: Chintz Bunny, Plump Polished Apple, Machine-Sewn Crazy, Amish Patchwork Kite, Rosebud Greetings, Pansy Cards, Ribbon Wreathed Heart*
- *Techniques: Basic Machine Appliqué on Cards, Crazy Quilting with Fancy Stitches, Stuffed Machine Appliqués, Machine Pieced Silhouettes, Making Ribbon Flowers for Cards*

Machine-stitched threads add instant interest and elegant detail to appliquéd greetings. Miraculously, it is easy to machine stitch paper! Fused cloth appliqués heat bonded to paper remain basic to this lesson in which machine stitchery adds a decorative embellishment. The very presence of high-tech stitching intrigues the viewer, surprises, and appeals to them. Imagine, sewn cards! Our card gallery photos sport both cards with plain threads (sewn in colors and in fancy stitches) and shiny metallic threads sewn in simple straight stitches. Whether you use a basic straight-stitch machine or one with fancy stitches, machine-made cards should tempt you.

* ARTWORK RECIPE 20:

Decorate a Silhouette Shaped Cut-out with a Fancy Stitch

The Chintz Bunny card (Fig. 7-1, Template 36) was heat bonded to page 1 of a Strathmore art paper card. A small circular tail in a low-contrast print was bonded in place over the bunny silhouette. One simple deco-rative zigzag stitch taken through page 1 only, finished and outlined the bunny. A different machine embroidery stitch makes a simple rectangular line around the card's perimeter, forming a border. This is machine appliqué on cards at its simplest and most traditional. In the card gallery photos you'll see Doris Gilbert's card where cloth squares bonded to a card make an impressionistic Christmas tree freely straight stitched in vertical lines resembling pine needles. Doris's approach is non-traditional but easy and effective!

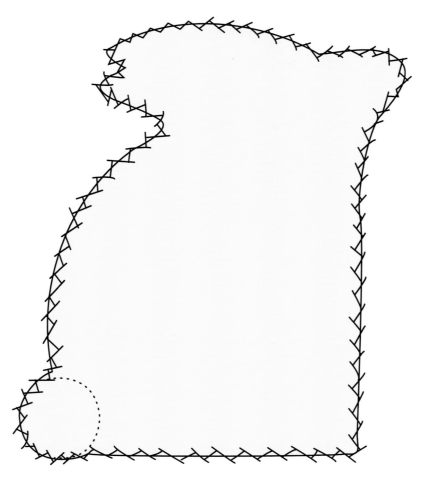

Fig. 7-1. *Template 36. Machine appliquéd rabbit by Debbie Niel.*

Card: *Plump and Shiny Polished Apple*

Since mythical times, apples have carried magic meanings. If you made up a dozen apple-embellished cards they would suit multiple card occasions and sentiments!

- Fold a 6" x 9" piece of white card stock in half so that it is 4½" x 6".
- From fused polished cotton cut one Template 38 (Fig. 7-2, p. 142) apple and leaf. Cut a second apple ¼" smaller all around out of a flat, thin, cotton batting. Sparingly, apply glue stick to the wrong side of the polished cotton apple.
- Position the appliqués on the card. Heat bond the leaf flat to the card. Fuse just ½" inside the edge of the apple, ironing around its outline. Pencil in the stems.
- With a tight and narrow zigzag stitch in a closely matching thread, sew over the apple's raw edge and the dip at the stem. The body of the apple will puff up plumply from this stitching.
- Stitch the edge of the leaf and the center veins in green. Satin stitch the stems in brown.
- White stitching shows inside the card on page 2, it is inoffensive to me. But if it concerns you, paste a paper heart over it.

Editorial Element: Inscribe the card inside: You are the apple of my eye! Or, Get Well Soon! Or, Congratulations on your Golden Apple! Or, Be Good to Yourself! (An apple a day, etc.)

Envelope Information: This card mails in a 4⅝" x 6½" envelope.

Card: *Crazy Quilt Heart.*

This is an elegant card and one that is easily mass produced.

- Card stock: Begin Fig. 7-3's, p. 142, heart card with a box of pastel Strathmore blank art cards.
- Crazy Quilt: Bond angular scraps of fused fabric to a fat quarter (18" x 22") of muslin or old sheet. Limit the number of colors, but vary the textures and fancy fabrics. This enhances the antique crazy quilt look. Bond this crazy patchwork to a fat quarter of thin, cotton batting. Iron a fat quarter of freezer paper to the uncovered batting surface to stiffen it and protect the feed on the machine.
- With decorative thread and fancy stitches, embellish all the seamlines. See Fig. 7-3, p. 142.
- Remove the freezer paper from the back of the crazy quilt.
- Cut as many Template 35 (Fig. 7-3) hearts out of this crazy quilted fat quarter as you can.
- Position the appliqué on page 1 of the card and adhere it with glue stick around the outer edge.
- Use a sturdy decorative stitch to sew the perimeter of the heart to the card.
- In the lower left, pencil in the number of the card like that on a hand printed picture (Heart, #3). Sign the card in the lower right like a painter (E. Sienkiewicz, 1997). Who could fail to be honored by receiving such a luxurious-looking card?

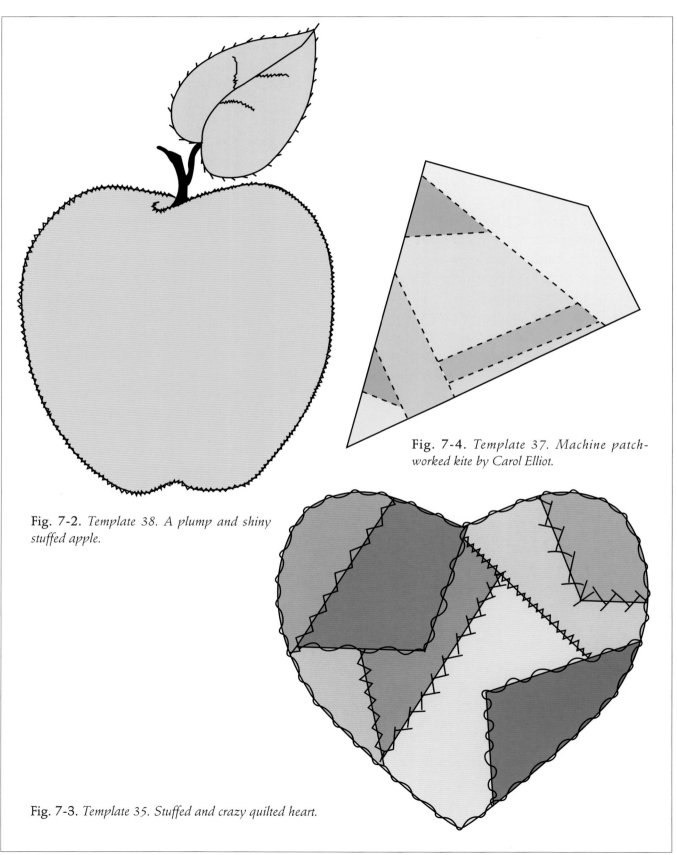

Fig. 7-2. *Template 38. A plump and shiny stuffed apple.*

Fig. 7-4. *Template 37. Machine patch-worked kite by Carol Elliot.*

Fig. 7-3. *Template 35. Stuffed and crazy quilted heart.*

* ARTWORK RECIPE 21:

Patchwork Silhouettes

To make the Amish-colored Kite pictured as Template 37 (Fig. 7-4), first fold an 8½" x 11" page of art stock into quarters. Cut the silhouette of a kite out of page 1, centering the design to your taste. Just as we made a fat quarter of crazy quilt fabric to mass produce the previous heart card, a fat quarter of patchwork can be pieced from scraps. For Template 37's card, a patchwork was made of intense Amish colors. From this patchwork 4" x 4" rectangles were cut and glued around their perimeter behind page 1's kite-shape window. The raw edges of this patchwork are hidden behind page 2. This card is so artful and so all-purpose that a set of these tied with ribbon would make a perfect bread-and-butter gift!

* ARTWORK RECIPE 22:

Patchwork Heart

Decorate the heart on page 144 by sewing machine using a basic, medium-long straight stitch and metallic thread. Both thread and stitching ornament this card. The thread is straight and tight where it is sewn, but loose and flowing where the tails hang freely. Put the same color thread in the bobbin as the thread in the top of the machine. Use gold, silver, or bronze thread. Try silky rayon thread in a softly shiny color, or stitch first with flat colors and then metallics. This stitching is more contemporary looking, more painterly, than the formal decoration achieved by a repeated embroidery stitch.

Card: Flashy Accordion-Folded Techno-fancy Heart!

This card's accordion heart is made from Template 38 and is pictured in Fig. 7-5A. For a cloth-covered accordion folded card, score the card stock before the appliqué is bonded to it. Then score a second time, through the fabric.

- Fold a 7" x 10" rectangle of red card stock in half.
- Cut a 4" x 5" rectangle of fused cloth and bond it to page 1 so that a ½" border shows around the top and the two sides of the background rectangle. Leave a larger margin at the bottom, to title the card.
- Cut a Template 38 (Fig. 7-5B) heart out of the same red card stock. Gold speckle the card stock with fine and bold gold pens.
- With a pencil, mark the mountain folds (dotted lines) and valley (dashed lines) folds shown on the template. Remember that the mountain lines are scored on the back side of the heart, the valley lines are scored on the front.
- Score the marked fold lines.
- With gold metallic thread in the top of the machine and in the bobbin and using a medium stitch-length, machine straight stitch the folds. Leave 3" starting and finishing threads to dangle freely over the heart .
- Squeeze the accordion pleats together.
- Draw a 2" diameter circle of white glue onto the center of page 1's

cloth rectangle.
- When the glue has dried a bit, position the folded heart over it.
- Inscribe this techno-fancy with

pride! For reasons of tradition, writing on page 1 with a soft black carbon pencil implies fine art. That seems appropriate here.

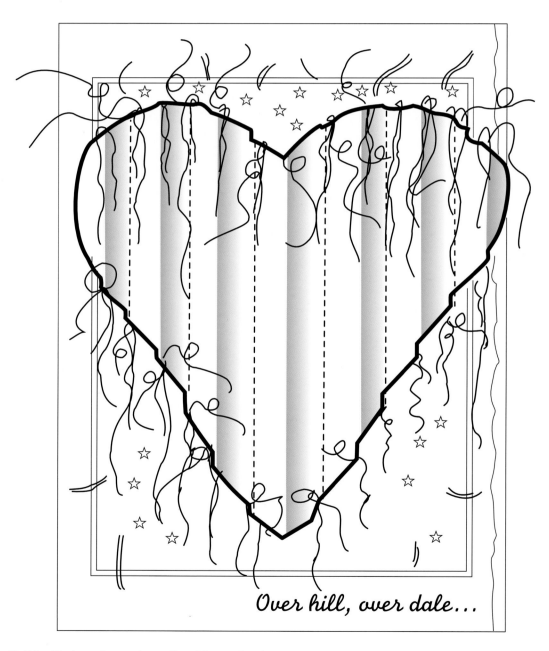

Over hill, over dale...

Fig. 7-5A. *Techno-fancy Accordion Heart Card. Inside: Through all life's ups and downs our love sustains me* ♡.

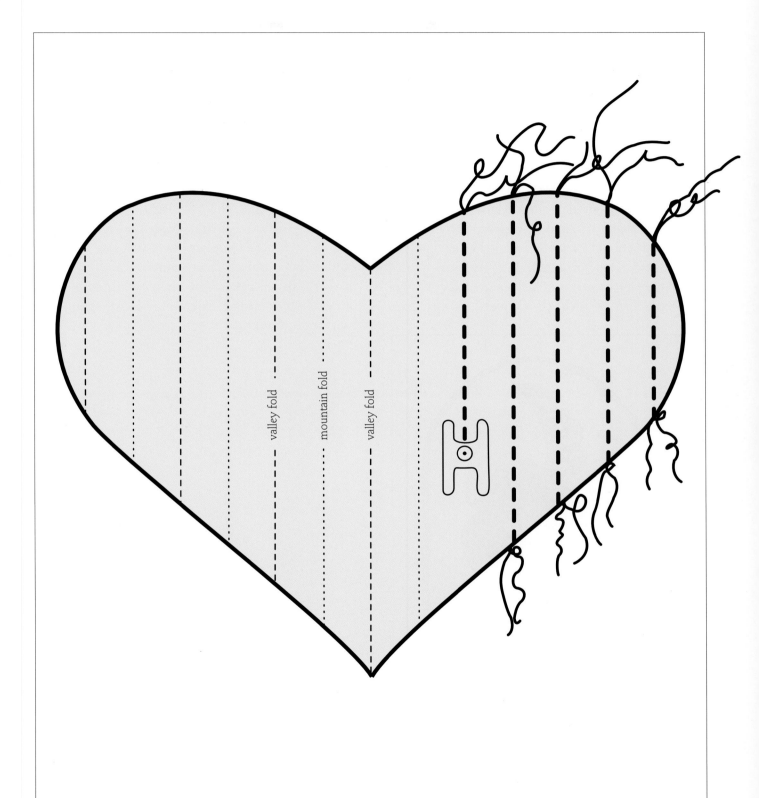

Fig. 7-5B. *Template 38. Accordion fold Heart card template.*

valley fold

mountain fold

valley fold

* ARTWORK RECIPE 23:

Ribbon Flower Cards

An easy and effective way to add both dimension and realism to a paper greeting is to glue on flowers made from shaded wired ribbon. This ribbon is available in floral, quilt, paper, and sewing shops. Made of acetate, its fine threads are shaded from light to dark and a tiny copper or steel wire is bound into the edging. This combination of realistic, almost painterly color, and the malleability of wire makes lovely ribbon flowers. A directory

teaching how to make simple wired ribbon flowers concludes this lesson. Yet more such flowers are taught in my earlier book, *Romancing Ribbons into Flowers*. You'll note that the process is spectacularly easy. Most often, the ribbon is gathered on one wire and closed, for cards, by stapling rather than by stitching. Then the finished flowers are glued to the cards.

The Pansy Cards are simple and graphic. Fig. 7-6 gives the templates for a window card with a glued button pansy center. Fig. 7-7B is a single-fold card which invites yarn stems and a doughnut-like daisy (Fig. 7-7A), again, with a button center.

Just sew you know that

Fig. 7-6. *Pansy Window Card. Inside: We're all hoping you'll soon be back in bloom!*

Fig. 7-7A. *How to Make a Ribbon Card Daisy:*
• *⅝" x 8½" shaded wired ribbon.*
• *Pull bottom wire to gather.*
• *Staple to form circle.*
• *Flatten circle. Glue to card. Glue button in center.*

Fig. 7-7B right. *Daisy Card. Inside (in the hearts): "health," "happiness," "congratulations!"*

bestwishes bestwishes

* ARTWORK RECIPE 24:

Rose & Rosebud Greetings

Roses and rosebuds are my favorite card flowers. The simplest rose to make is the pin rose, page 153 in the Directory of Simple Dimensional Flowers. These roses are flat and easily glued to the card. Ink embellishment to stem, leaves, and flower quickly marks them as the Victorians' beloved Moss Rose.

Rosebuds cut from a circle, folded, and gathered (Fig. 7-8A–D) are a flower I designed back in 1987 for revivalist Baltimore Album Quilts. I love them still! Please note that in making a rosebud greeting the leaf, stem, and calyx (just up to Template 39's dotted line) are ironed down first. Then the bud is made and glued behind the calyx. Next the top of the calyx is heat bonded over the bud. The finishing touch is fine ink work done in Pigma Micron .01 black pen.

Fig. 7-9. *Template 39.*

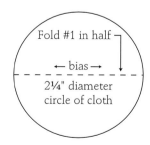

Fig. 7-8A. *Making a rosebud.*

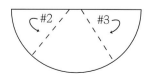

Fig. 7-8B. *Fold circle in half, then into sixths.*

Fig. 7-8C. *Running stitch through all layers and pull to gather.*

Fig. 7-8D. *Insert rosebud under calyx. Heat bond calyx to rosebud.*

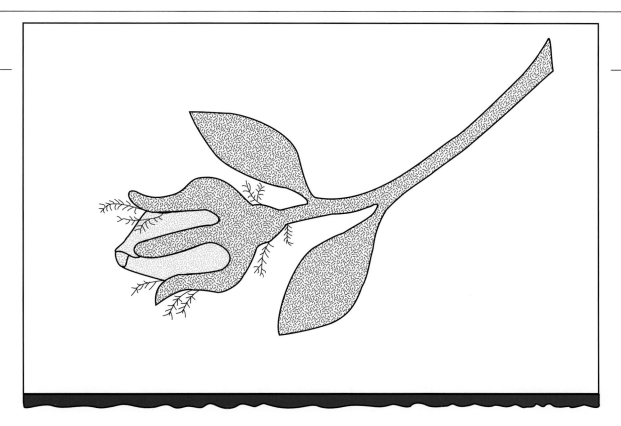

Fig. 7-10 above. *Template 40.*   **Fig. 7-11 below.** *Template 41.*

Card 7-1. *Cachepot of Pansies, pillow top, made by Elly Sienkiewicz. Pattern shown on page 187.*

Card 7-2, right. *Ribbon Wreathed Heart made by Elly Sienkiewicz.*

Fig. 7-12. *The Ribbon Wreathed Heart Card.*

Appliqué Paper Greetings – Elly Sienkiewicz

Ribbon Wreathed Heart

The Ribbon Wreathed Heart (Fig. 7-12) should be inscribed with something memorable and then framed under glass! In a stiff plastic mailer — the kind with pleated sides and a string-wrap tie — it could also be mailed without a frame as a card. For very special occasions I've made such grand-scale cards. One favorite is to make a vase or urn of flowers. Clusters of flowers open as separate cards with individual wishes. You'll spot this Victorian complexity in the color photos on page 113. The ribbon wreathed heart (Fig. 7-12) is shown to size and all its flowers are taught in the Directory of Simple Dimensional Flowers which follows.

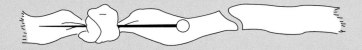

Directory of Simple Dimensional Flowers

PIN ROSE

Supplies
- *A long quilter's or corsage pin*
- *18" length of ⅝" wide shaded wired ribbon*

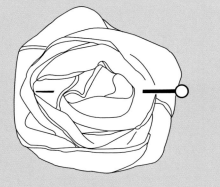

Fig. A.

- Tie a loose over-hand knot at the left-hand end of the 18" ribbon.
- Gently wind the ribbon clockwise under and around the pin (Fig. A). Tuck the tail under the rose.
- On the "underside" seal the rose's shape with white glue. Remove pin (Fig. B).

Fig. B.

DIMENSIONAL CALICO LEAVES

Supplies
- *Three ovate leaves cut from fused green cloth*
- *Stapler*

- Fold the leaf in half, right sides together (Fig. C).
- Staple in a small tuck.
- Iron the open leaf to bond it to the card.
- Use gold ink to embellish the leaves with serrate margins and veins (Fig. D).

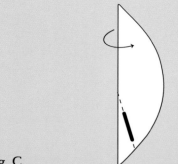

Fig. C.

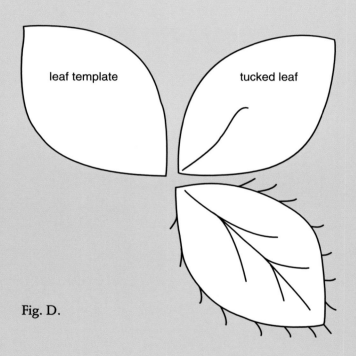

leaf template

tucked leaf

Fig. D.

RIBBON LEAVES

Leaf A — Supplies
- *⅞" wide x 2½" long ribbon*

- Fold the leaf as shown in diagram (Fig. E).
- Running stitch.
- Pull to gather to a width of ¾".
- Trim off excess below gathers.
- Embellish with gold pen (Fig. F).

fold

1. 2.

Fig. E.

Fig. F.

Leaf B — Supplies

- *⅝" wide x 3" long ribbon*

- Fold the leaf as shown in Fig. G.
- Fold the leaf as shown in Fig. H.
- Staple a pleat in leaf's center. The staple will be covered by another leaf or by a flower glued over that portion of the leaf (Fig. I).
- *Optional:* Embellish with gold pen (Fig. J).

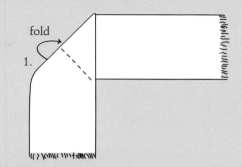

Fig. G.

Fig. H.   **Fig. I.**   **Fig. J.**

Leaf C — Supplies

- *⅞" wide x 3" long ribbon*

- Fold the leaf as shown in Fig. K.
- Fold the leaf as shown in Fig. L.
- Staple a pleat in the center. The staple will be covered by another leaf or flower glued over that portion of the leaf (Fig. M).

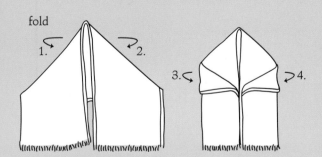

Fig. K.   **Fig. L.**

Leaf D

- *⅞" wide x 3" long ribbon*

- Leaf D is the underside of Leaf C (Fig. M).

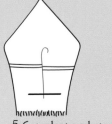

5. ↪ pleat and staple

Fig. M.

Bud E — Supplies
- *⅞" wide x 3" long ribbon*

- Fold the bud as shown in Fig. N.
- Roll from right to left (Fig. O).
- When the strip is rolled from a to b, press the top center forward and down. Staple the base (Fig. P).

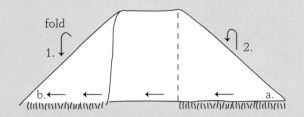

Fig. N.

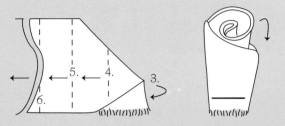

Fig. O. **Fig. P.**

Bud F in Calyx
- *2 lengths — ⅞" wide x 3" long green ribbon*

- Use Leaf D to wrap around Bud E.
- Pull base in to the center, gathering it slightly. Staple (Fig. Q).

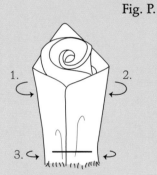

Fig. Q.

Alternate Calyx G
- *2 lengths — ⅞" wide x 3" long ribbon*

- Wrap a finished Bud E in ribbon folded as if starting Bud E (Fig. R).
- Pull base in to the center, gathering it slightly. Staple (Fig. S).

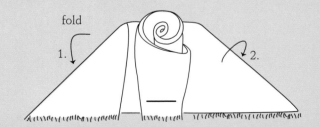

Fig. R.

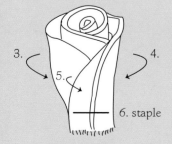

Fig. S.

CARD FLOWER BASICS

Flower H — Supplies
- *Shaded wired ribbon (⅝" x 4½"; ⅞" x 5½") is the easiest ribbon to use. Satin works, too.*

- Gather the ribbon on the inside wire (the base of the flower) by pulling the ribbon down. Hold the ribbon in a U-shape, grasping both ends of the wire at once. Gather as tightly as possible (Fig. T).
- Fold the ribbon in half, twisting the wires to hold the gathers tightly (Fig. U).
- "Seam" the flower with two staples. Fold the top ¼" seam over and down at a 45° angle (Fig. U).
- Hide the seam at the back of the flower (Fig. V).
- Hide the bottom gather wire by pushing the front of the flower down to form an open cup. Then glue to card (Fig. V).

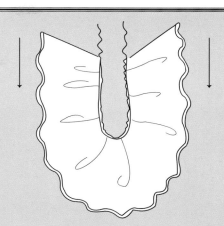

Fig. T.

Fig. U.

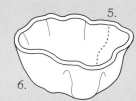

Fig. V.

Flower I — Supplies
- *⅞" wide x 6½" long shaded wired ribbon*

- Gather the ribbon tightly, on the bottom wire.
- Fold the ribbon as in the diagram (Fig. W).
- Roll the flower into a relatively loose coil, rolling from point a on the right to point b on the left (Fig. W).
- The finished flower is about 1½" in diameter. Glue it to the card with its gathered edge tucked under the "cup" (Fig. X).

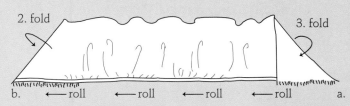

Fig. W.

Fig. X.

Flower J — Supplies
- *1½" wide x 7" long shaded wired ribbon*

- This flower is made the same as Flower I. However, after the second and third step and before it is rolled, a ¼" cuff is folded away from the maker (Fig. Y).
- The resulting flower is topped by a ¼" cuff around the top edge (Fig. Z).

Fig. Y.

the cuff →

Fig. Z.

Flower K — Supplies
- *1½" wide x 5½" long shaded wired ribbon*

- Gather the bottom wire tightly and twist the two pulled wires together.
- One third of the way down from the top edge, place a running stitch from right to left, the length of the ribbon. Pull to gather. Secure the thread (Fig. AA).
- Twist the top wires together. Staple the seam.
- Glue the trumpet-like flower to the card, all seams hidden beneath it.
- The resulting flower is topped by a ¼" ruffle around the top edge (Fig. BB).

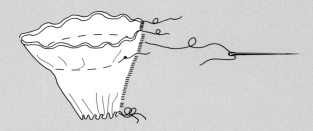

Fig. AA.

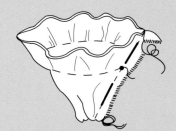

Fig. BB.

Fringed Center — Supplies

- 1½" x 1½" shaded ribbon, wires removed.
- Cut a square of ribbon (Fig. CC).
- Fold it in half diagonally.
- Pull ⅓" of thread out on all four sides to imitate flower stamens (Fig. DD).
- Dab glue in center of flower to hold this center in place (Fig. EE).

Beaded Centers

- Gold, yellow, or bronze seed beads can be glued to flower centers.

Ink Embellishments

- The heart-wreathed card is embellished in fine point gold metallic pen (Pentel®). The embellishing motifs are leaves, ferns, serrate leaf edgings, veins, rose moss, grapes, and tendrils. Seed beads (gold) are glued on for added texture and dimension.

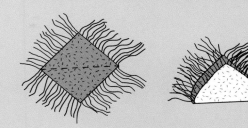

Fig. CC.   Fig. DD.

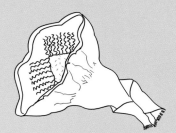

Fig. EE.

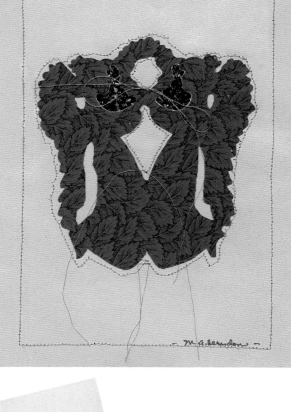

Card 7-3. *Made by Elly Sienkiewicz.*

Card 7-4, right. *Made by Mary Ann Herndon.*

Card 7-5. *Made by Elly Sienkiewicz.*

Card 7-6. *Made by Susan McKelvey.*

Gratitude

Card 7-8. *Made by Elly Sienkiewicz.*

Card 7-7. *Made by Doris Gilbert.*

Card 7-9. *Made by Doris Gilbert.*

Card 7-10. *Made by Kathy Galos.*

Appliqué Paper Greetings — Elly Sienkiewicz

Masterful Presentations & Fabulous Finales from Greetings to Gifts

- *Masterful Presentations: Envelopes, Gift Bags, Boxes, and Gift Tags Ornamented by Cloth-on-Paper Appliqués*
- *Fabulous Finales: Framable Quilted Cards, Wedding Wishes Card, and Wedding Pillow; Friendship's Offering Card and Pillow, Cache-pot of Pansies, Framable Card and Pillow, Country Angel Stand-Up Card and Soft Doll, Froggy Stand-Up Card and Beanbag; Decorative Hanging Mobiles; and a Birthday Banner to festoon a loved one's special day.*

There is a fine art to giving a gift, be it a card or something more substantial. The art is in the presentation. Today, the burgeoning of shops specializing in paper supplies, party goods, and greeting cards offer aids to dramatic gift presentation. There are colored tissue papers, cellophane tissue, elaborate stickers, sparkles, and spangles to slip into an envelope, bag, or box, and a richness of ribbons. The style possibilities range from frilly Victorian opulence to high-tech plastics and metallics. These fruits of capitalism so tempt us that the packaging of a gift can add substantially to its cost. Yet, with cloth-on-paper appliqué, unique presentation is at your fingertips, relegating the addition of store-bought accoutrements to an optional splurge.

Through these Paper Greeting lessons, a sense of your own style will have developed. Whatever your style, you are sure to be a master of presentation! This lesson highlights cloth on paper in ornamenting envelopes, bags, boxes, and gift tags. It concludes with Fabulous Finales: card designs which translate into more substantial gifts.

GIFT GREETINGS:

Masterful Presentations: Envelopes, Mailers, Gift Bags, Tags, and Boxes,

Envelopes

Making envelopes is straightforward. Envelopes consist of a solid front. Four flaps overlap in the back to close the envelope. Sometimes the back flaps are basically triangles. Sometimes they are basically rectangles. Like cards, the envelope's material makes all the difference. When you use colored art paper, the envelope looks rich even without ornamentation. Shelf paper or drawing paper envelopes, decorated with heat-bonded appliqués, look special. Fabric bonded to any kind of paper and mailed as a cloth envelope cannot fail to honor its recipient! The simplest way to learn how to make an envelope is to pry apart (or cautiously steam open) a purchased envelope of the desired size. Open it flat and use it as a pattern. Use it as the template to cut the same envelope shape out of card stock or art paper. Or use it as the template to which you fuse an ornamental fabric covering. Then follow these steps:

- Lay the cut, unfolded envelope on the table, wrong side (inside) up.
- Following the fold lines marked on the template, score the four valley folds.
- Fold the left and right side flaps in first. Paint the lower half of the triangle's margins with rubber cement. Paint it on the outside of the envelope in a strip about ⅓" wide.
- Similarly, paint the inside of the bottom flap's margins with rubber cement. Allow a few seconds for the glue to get tacky.

- Fold up the bottom flap and press firmly to seal it against the overlapped side flaps.

Variations: Ornamentation is becoming increasingly common on envelopes. Drawn or printed decoration seems to present no problem with the U.S. Postal Service. Postal code states that pasted on decorations must be securely fastened around all edges. In the most elegant of envelopes, the top flap is cut into a decorative symmetrical design. Other variations include bonding a diamond-shaped cloth appliqué onto the inside of an envelope's upper flap and opening. Tailor the diamond to a purchased envelope and have the cloth echo that on the enclosed card.

Mailers

Jazzy modern mailers abound! Mailers which hold the standard 8½" x 11" letter size paper come in translucent plastic, in shiny card stock, in metallic plastic bubble wrap, as well as in serviceable brown and white appropriate for fused-cloth ornamentation. Padded envelopes or mailers are available both smaller and larger than the letter size mailers. The fiber-filled ones take heat-bonded appliqués nicely. Of course, the plastic, bubble-lined ones should not be ironed. The ready-made letter size cardboard express mailers provided by the Postal Service, U.P.S., and Federal Express can all be heat-bonded with cloth, either covered with it or ornamented with appliqués. Stationery and office supply stores also carry plain cardboard photo mailers which invite paper appliqué.

Gift Bags: A Gift Bag with Handles and Matching Tag

We all love a handled gift bag for its ease. You just pop the gift into it. Nesting the bag first with colored tissue is popular since its crisp corners peek out temptingly. Curled paper bows can be tied onto the handle. Use the bows to secure a paper appliqué tag coordinated to the bag. Unfortunately, the expense of the prettiest gift bags — the printed ones and those made of shiny paper — mounts quickly. But not if you decorate the bags yourself! The least expensive approach is to buy plain bags in bulk from a paper wholesaler. Look up paper or labels or packaging in your Yellow Pages. Or scout the local gift and card shops. That is where I found a local distributor: *"Elman Labels and Paper Products, Silver Spring, MD; 301-588-8292"* was printed on the bottom of several different types of bags. To order, I purchased in bulk a size useful both for teaching *Appliqué Paper Greetings* classes and for gift giving. This size was 7⅝" x 9¾" x 4¾" deep and came in both bright white and brown. You may have a specialized need which calls for a smaller or a larger bag. You can call your distributor and ask for his catalog which will give specific sizes and possibly other *Appliqué Paper Greetings* supplies as well.

Bags with handles pack flat. You can decorate the front with any iron-on cloth appliqué. Any of the patterns from this book could be used for ornamentation. Consider also a collage of round or heart-shaped balloons with loose, cut ribbon strings hanging out from underneath. Try patchwork patterns, Sunbonnet Sues, other simple appliqué designs, or uncomplicated Baltimore Album appliqué wreath patterns.

Cloth-Covered Gift Bags

You can easily cloth cover a small square-bottom gift bag of a size that could hold a piece of jewelry or a wrapped chunk of fudge. You could also cloth cover a bottle bag to give a bottle of wine or flavored vinegar, or cut it down a bit to present a pint jar of condiments. Simply use a brown paper bag of suitable size as the template. Carefully take it apart. If it is intact, use it as the framework on which to bond the cloth. If it is not whole, it can still be used to reconstruct the bag's shape. Cut this pattern out of a heavyweight, brown grocery bag, shelf, or drawing paper. Fuse the fabric to the outside of the bag shape so that the folds you score into the paper are valley ones. Use rubber cement to seal the fused paper into the bag shape. If you use a pretty print, stripe, or plaid, these bags really need no additional ornament.

Gifted Boxes

Any box which collapses flat can be decorated with heat-bonded appliqués. Department store gift-wrap centers carry folded boxes, as do bakeries. If you want to make up large batches of cloth-covered boxes, try purchasing the basic boxes from a local wholesale paper and packaging source. Betty Alderman's farm scene box, pictured on page 136, suggests a wealth of possibilities not just for decorated boxes, but for boxes as gift greetings in themselves! Betty has also fashioned a town house which suggests the creation of an entire snow-covered village made from boxes and displayed on a mantle. But box decoration can be as simple as covering a small box in cloth or bonding on a decoration of cloth appliqués.

Pizza Album Block Box: A useful gift for someone making an appliquéd Album Quilt is a decorated box (previously an unused pizza box) in which she can safely store her Album blocks in progress. Open the box flat and on the wrong side (the unprinted side) bond your ornament. This idea comes from Stephanie J.

Bradskey who makes a fused heart-and-hand appliquéd box for each student who successfully completes her beginning Baltimore album quilt course. Fused cloth can also be bonded over the pizza parlor's printed message. Refold the box so that the unprinted side is the outside. Sometimes the inside is brown cardboard which when appliquéd has a charming country look.

Recycle Suggestion: Save cylindrical containers such as those that hold oatmeal or cocoa. These can be decorated for giving baked goods at holiday time. A cylindrical container can be capped with a circle of pinked fabric, rubber-banded, then ribbon tied. While you cannot appliqué with heat to the cylinder's sides, you can to this circular cap. The container's sides can be paper-covered or covered with cloth fused to paper, then wrapped around the cylinder, overlapped, and glued.

FABULOUS FINALES: GIFT GREETINGS
* ARTWORK RECIPE 26:

Graphic Designs as Appliquéd Paper Greetings, as Quilted Cards, as Stuffed Tree Ornaments, or as Framable Art

Some stylizations so delight us that they stay with us, finding reincarnation over the years as different objects. Some 30 years ago, before I went to housekeeping, I made small stuffed, felt Christmas tree ornaments for my hope chest. Two favorites were made from the decorative sheep pictured in Fig. 8-1. If you'd like to make yourself a pair, blow this pattern up by 120% on the photocopier, draw

each sheep's outline on felt, add ¼" seam allowance all around and cut out two of each sheep. Embroider the flowers and features, seam the front to the back leaving 1½" open along the base. Stuff, then stitch the opening closed. Make an embroidery floss hanging loop to carry a metal ornament hook.

Quilted Cards: These soft cards mail with a first class stamp in a standard business size envelope. They are so appealing that they could easily be mounted on art paper, set inside a raised mat board, and framed under non-glare glass. To make Fig. 8-1 or Fig. 8-2, p. 168, trace the design with a Pigma Micron .01 pen onto a 5" x 10" muslin or light-colored print cotton cloth. Work from a photocopy pinned beneath the cloth and use a light box if necessary. For color use Pigma Micron® Brush Pens combined with Sakura Calligraphic pens for the widest color range. Both are permanent. When the card's front is done, baste it to a same-size piece of thin batting and backing cloth. Hand quilt the card, then trim off the excess, just beyond the outside margin so that the cut edge softens with handling and the quilt sandwich of the card's construction is apparent.

Card 8-1. *Christmas ornament from using Fig. 8-1, made by Elly Sienkiewicz.*

seam line

quilting line →

Fig. 8-1. *Quilted card.*

Thank You!

Thinking of You!

Hooray!

Get Well Soon!

Love is My Love!

Happy Spring!

Lesson 8

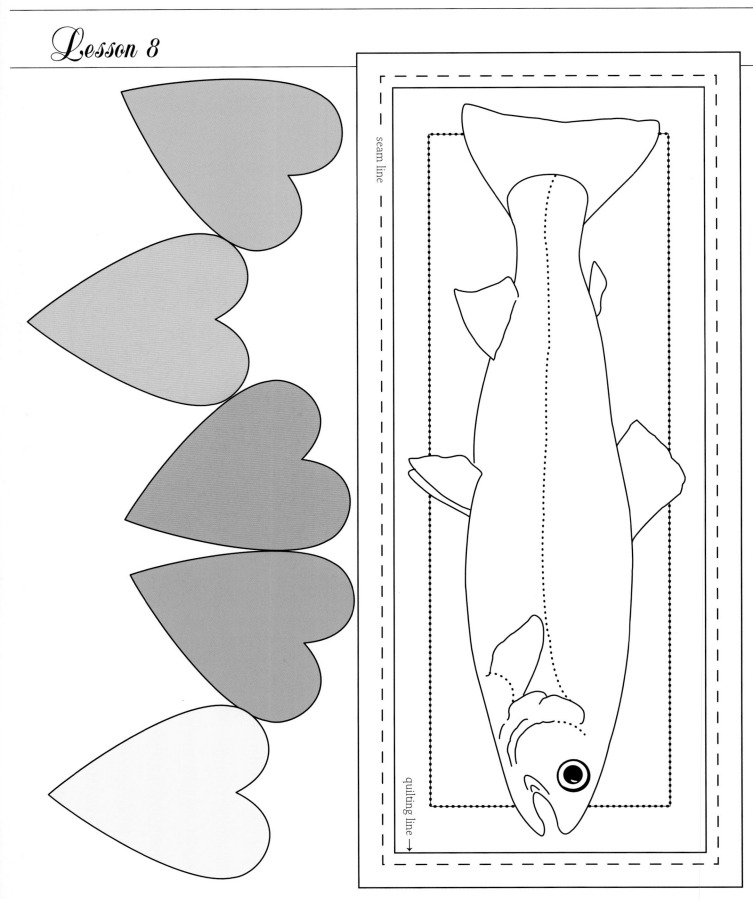

Fig. 8-2A. *Hearts for quilted card.*

Fig. 8-2B. *Quilted card.*

seam line

quilting line →

Appliqué Paper Greetings — Elly Sienkiewicz

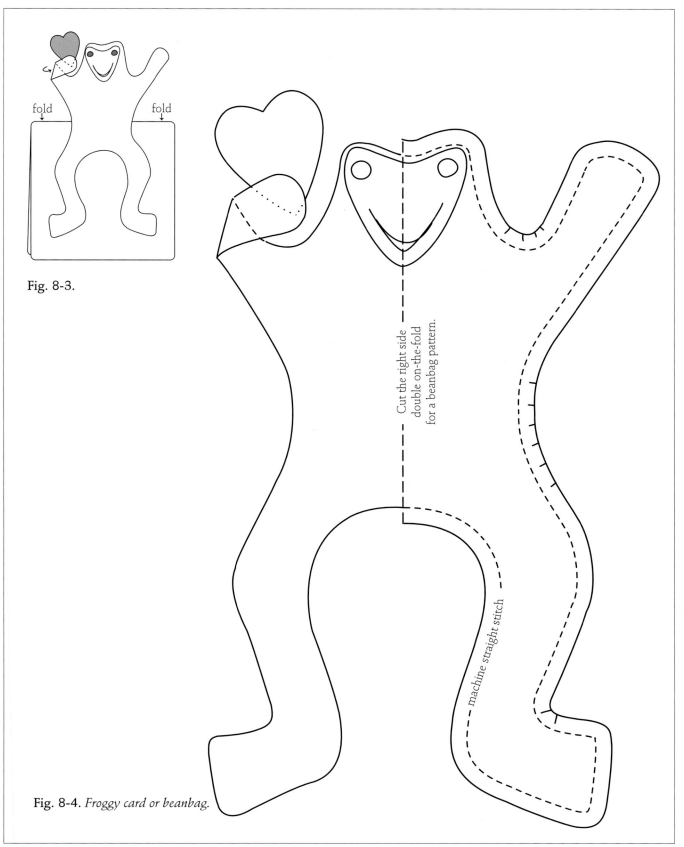

fold   fold

Fig. 8-3.

Cut the right side double on-the-fold for a beanbag pattern.

machine straight stitch

Fig. 8-4. *Froggy card or beanbag.*

* ARTWORK RECIPE 27:

Froggy Stand-Up Card and Beanbag

When I was quite grown up, I was given a creature beanbag. It brought back happy memories and drapes gracefully among my pillows. Beanbags give tactile pleasure and are a bit mysterious. One always wants to know what weighty and mobile stuff is hidden inside them! Fig. 8-3, p. 169, shows a folded stand-up card made from the beanbag pattern in Fig. 8-4, p. 169. To fashion a beanbag, make a pattern by cutting Fig. 8-4 double on-the-fold. Draw it onto the top of two layers (front and back, right-sides pinned together) of a gay and graphic print. As you cut this frog shape out, add a ¼" seam allowance all around. Fashion the face out of felt or Ultra-Suede® and ink or embroider the features. With a tight machine stitch, attach the frog's front (with face in place) to its back, right sides together, leaving 1½" of seam open between the legs. Turn the froggy right side out. Stuff this all-ages toy with two cups (or to taste) of dried pinto or navy beans and whipstitch the opening closed. To make the beanbag into a greeting, tie an inscribed heart tag (card stock or two cotton hearts fused together) to a front leg. Imagine the uplifting messages this froggy could carry!

* ARTWORK RECIPE 28:

Uncle Jack's Horse: Card and Soft Sculpture

Do some of your fond childhood memories attach to an object which now resides in someone else's home? Sometimes I pay such a thing homage by reproducing a version of it for my own. My grandfather, Uncle Jack, had from his childhood an ancient cloth horse stuffed with straw. On wobbly legs, it stood about 11" tall from hooves to ears. First my grandmother, then my mother, brought this toy out lovingly each Christmas to spend the holiday with us, under the lowest tree branches. It seemed a magic thing, silent and venerable, balding a bit more with each season, like my grandfather himself. The card pictured in Fig. 8-5 shows my version of Uncle Jack's horse.

Christmas Horse Soft Sculpture: Fig. 8-6 pictures the simple patchwork from which a standing soft-sculpture horse can be made. Fig. 8-6 instructs how you can have the horse figure enlarged at the printer to pattern size. Cut this pattern out of freezer paper and iron it lightly to the right side of the patchwork. Draw around the pattern with a light color pencil, but do not cut the shape out yet. Make a quilt sandwich with the patchwork on the top, muslin on the bottom, and thin batting in between. Quilt the body of the horse, stitching to ⅛" beyond the drawn outline. When the quilting is finished, cut out the horse shape, adding a ¼" seam. Pin the quilted front right sides together to a black cotton backing, then cut the back to the same size as the front. Using a tight machine stitch, sew front to back leaving a 2" opening along the belly seam. Reinforce inside curves and corners, then clip to ⅔ their depth.

Fig. 8-5. *Patchwork Christmas Horse Card.*

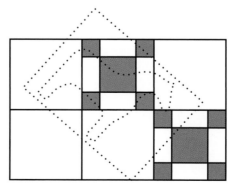

Fig. 8-6. *For card the small patchwork corner squares are 1". For the Soft Sulpture Horse, have your printer enlarge Fig. 8-5 and Fig. 8-6 so that the small corner squares are 3" square.*

Finishing and mounting the horse soft sculpture: Turn the body right side out. Stuff the horse tightly. Insert a ⅓" diameter x 10" long wooden dowel about 3" into the horse, entering at the center of the belly seam. Test that your placement will hold the horse straight (parallel to the table). Carefully drizzle white glue around the insertion. When it has dried, stitch the belly seam closed. Loop rusty red knitting yarn for the mane and tail. Drill a ½" wide x 2" deep hole in the top center of a 4" x 5" x 6" rectangle of treated or weathered lumber. Fill the hole with a bit of wood glue. Insert the dowel into this, wipe away the excess, and let it dry. Sign and date this museum-like mounting block. Stable the horse under your Christmas tree! Should you perhaps make several? Some young person you love may watch your horse silently year after year, attaching to it the magic of his own holiday memories. You might even inscribe this gifted greeting in verse: "Sit this horse under your tree. As Christmas passes, remember me."

* ARTWORK RECIPE 29:

Friendship's Offering Card and Pillow

When seeking a logo for the Elly Sienkiewicz Appliqué Academy, I drew up a particularly easy graphic design (Fig. 8-7). While the original was made into the conference pin, it also makes a fine card (Fig. 8-7) and a charming gift pillow (Fig. 8-8). The word Friendship is cut from the calligraphy cloth in the Baltimore Beauties® by Elly Sienkiewicz designer collection for P & B Textiles. While this fabric is widely available, you could inscribe the heart with anything. A colleague,

Fig. 8-7. *Friendship's Offering Pillow.*

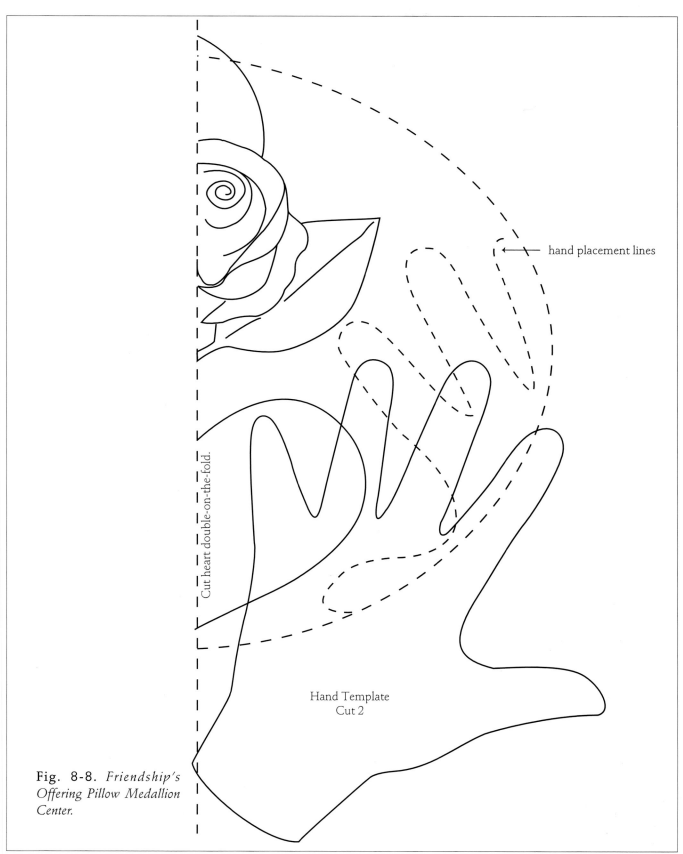

hand placement lines

Cut heart double-on-the-fold.

Hand Template
Cut 2

Fig. 8-8. *Friendship's Offering Pillow Medallion Center.*

Wendy Grande, is making an utterly elegant appliquéd, embroidered, ribbon-embellished, Baltimore-style album quilt. What has she written in ornately bold calligraphy in the center of this late twentieth-century classic? Carefully scripted in a quilted diamond is "Get Real!"

Wendy's bravado should inspire us all to give our art and even our pillows the coin of their times. Some pundit has observed that only if we give our art the coin of its times can it speak to the present and so to the future. I want to border Fig. 8-8 in some elegant nineteenth-century reproduction prints and inscribe its heart with "Cope," "Cultivate Thy Soul," or "Breathe in calm. Breathe out and smile." I would like to make these pillows for several dear ones.

To make Friendship's Offering into a pillow: Fig. 8-8's pattern elements are bonded to a 9" x 12" rectangle. Cut the foundation to 12" – 14" square if you prefer a pillow. Layer in this order: 1. the oval; 2. the heart; 3. the hands. The rose is a pin rose (Lesson 7) made from two feet of ⅞" wide shaded, wire ribbon. Its leaves are from an inexpensive "silk" artificial flower, stitched down. The rose stem and the outline of the heart are outline stitched and embroidered in 4mm silk ribbon. Blanket stitch in overdyed pearl cotton outlines the heart. Borders with corner squares can be sewn on to the patterned medallion to build the pillow top up to the desired size. Pillow forms are easier to use than loose stuffing, so decide the finished size with a purchased pillow form in hand. Ideally, complete the pillow as a slip-cover that can be removed for washing rather than stitching it shut over the pillow form.

* ARTWORK RECIPE 30:

Country Angel Stand-Up Card and Soft Doll

(See the card and the doll, Fig. 8-9 and Fig. 8-10, p. 177.)

Years ago with three young children still at home, I started Cabin Fever Calicoes, a quilt shop by mail. It ran for a while after I sold it in 1984, but the third owner closed its doors. During the seven years I owned it, one of the things I enjoyed the most was writing the catalog's opening letter to the customers and coming up with small treats to thank them for ordering. The Country Angel was one such pattern I designed. She had a life of her own and pleased patrons sent me snapshots of her made up as a bride and as a fairy. My eldest son, not yet a teenager, wrote a story about the Country Angel watching over a big country house in Maine, keeping it clean and safe while the family was away during the winter. The Country Angel makes a charming paper doll card with a kick stand for support (Fig. 8-9). She also makes a sweetly simple, soft doll gift.

Country Angel Doll:
MATERIALS

FABRIC

Body: 13" x 22½" piece of flesh color or muslin cotton

Gown: 12" x 22½" piece of white, gauzy voile

Smock: 12" x 9" piece of taupe polished cotton

Wings, heart: 6½" x 23" piece of strawberry polished cotton

Heart: 4" x 6" piece of deep rose polished cotton

Hearts: 4" x 6" piece of wine red polished cotton

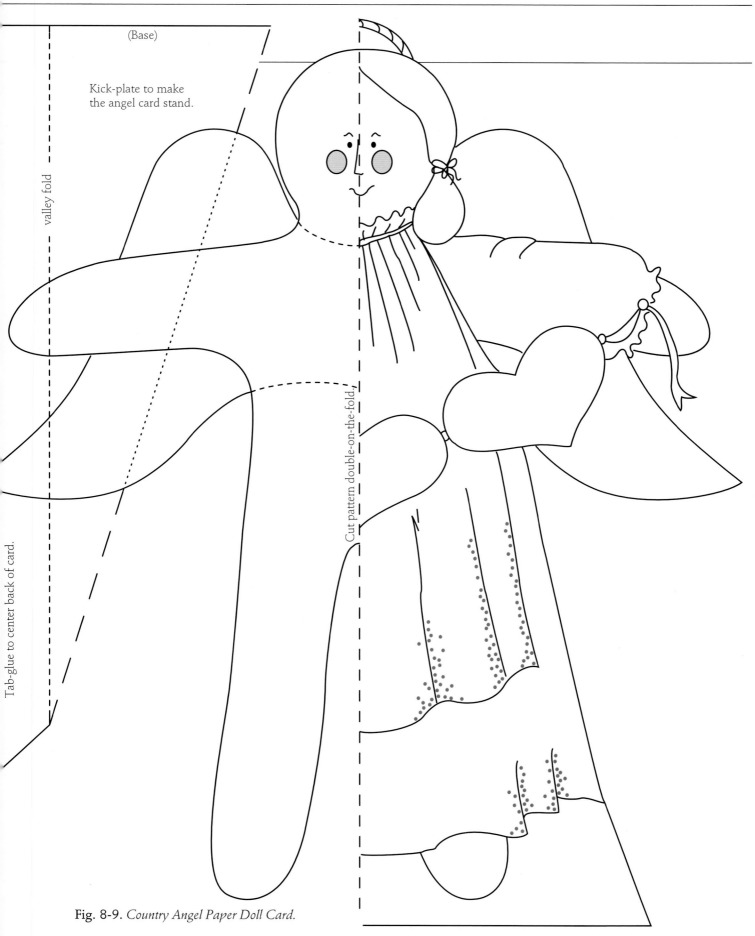

(Base)

Kick-plate to make
the angel card stand.

valley fold

Tab-glue to center back of card.

Cut pattern double-on-the-fold.

Fig. 8-9. *Country Angel Paper Doll Card.*

Ribbon: ⅛" x 12" wine red, satin ribbon for threading hearts

Gold Cord for halo: 6" of twisted gold cord trim

Embroidery Floss: Two skeins of warm brown or other hair color

Features: Pigma Micron® .01 black pen, red ball point, or variegated red sewing thread

Filler: Polyester fiberfil to stuff the body, thin quilt batting to fill the wings

Procedure: Cut the Fig. 8-10 patterns for the angel body and wings, double on-the-fold. Pin the body pattern to two layers of flesh colored cotton. Trace the outline on the top layer, then cut the doll out adding ¼" seam as you do. Before you stitch front and back together, lightly pencil the facial features on both. That way you have a second chance if you mess up when going over the first face's eye, nose, and mouth in black Pigma Micron .03 pen.

Face: Fill the cheeks in with lightly drawn, red ballpoint. Test the process first! Alternatively, fill the cheek outline in with concentric circles of a variegated pink, single sewing thread.

The super soft-sculpture secret is to sew around the entire shape with a tight machine stitch and reinforce the clipped inside curves and corners. Then, in a place where it won't show, slash a 2" line through one layer. Use this hole to turn the shape right side out and to stuff the doll before whipstitching it closed. Stuff her midriff fairly loosely if you want her to sit, but very tightly if you want her to fly.

Hair: Gently slip the paper wrapper off hair-colored embroidery floss, leaving the skein intact. Tack the midpoint of the skein to the top center of her head, making a part. Tack down the floss at each ear, making two dog tails. Or coil it to make two more stately buns. Tack the second skein of floss in a coil to cover the back of her head. Sew on a circle of gold cord peeping over her head.

Wings: Add a ¼" seam to the pattern shape. Sew the wing fronts to the backs onto a layer of thin batting. Make a 1½" vertical slit between the wings in what will be the top cloth layer (the side sewn to the body). Turn the wings right side out, then outline quilt them. Quilt a small heart on each one. If you want to add an embroidery floss loop to hang her on the top of a Christmas tree, the time to stitch it is now! The wings will be fastened to the body after the angel is dressed.

Gown: Cut the fabric as illustrated in Fig. 8-11, p. 178. Then sew the sleeves into the slashed arm holes. Next sew the back of the gown closed (right sides together), leaving a 2" neck opening. Sew the top of each sleeve seam closed. Turn the gown right side out and machine hem the neck opening, sleeve edges, and bottom of gown. Do this as you would a scarf, turning under ¼", then ¼" again so that no raw edge shows. Dress your angel and hand gather the neck and sleeve cuffs closed. Secure stitches to finish.

Smock: Make this in the same way as the gown. Hem the armhole slashes, neck, back edges, and the smock's hem. Then hand gather the smock to her with running stitches, closing the shoulder point as you go. Tack closed at the neck, but leave the back open. Gather just below the ¼" hem so that a ruffle forms at the neck.

Garland of Hearts: Stuff four tiny hearts in several shades of red, plus enough of the wing color to tie the doll together visually. Thread a soft-sculpture (doll maker's) needle with ⅛" ribbon and knot through the angel's hand. Sew through and knot between each heart. Leave a 3" ribbon streamer at each end.

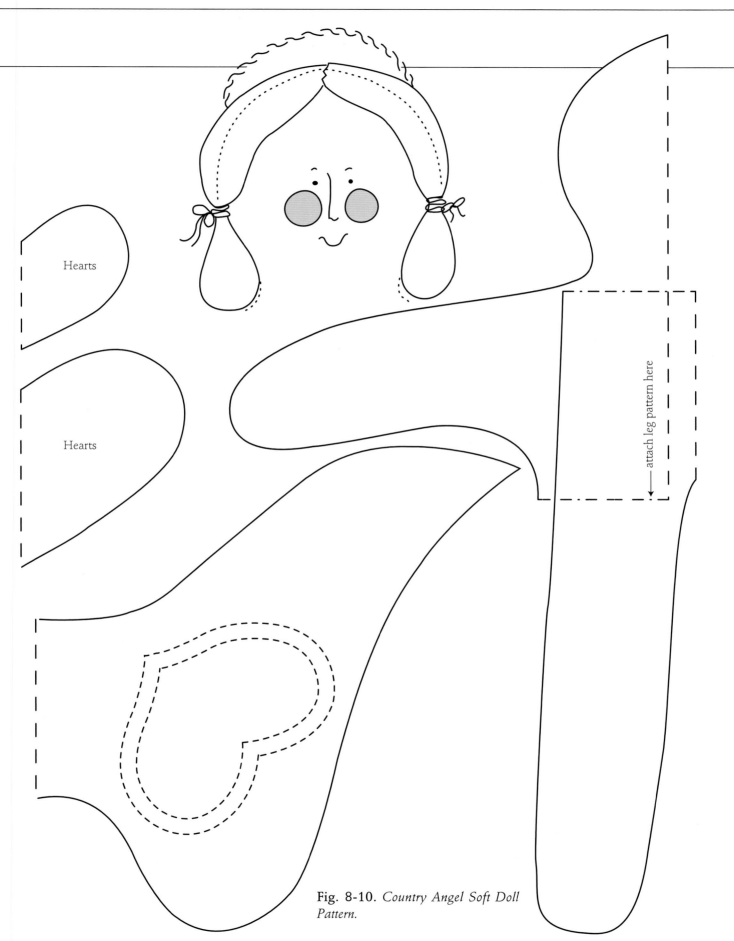

Hearts

Hearts

attach leg pattern here

Fig. 8-10. *Country Angel Soft Doll Pattern.*

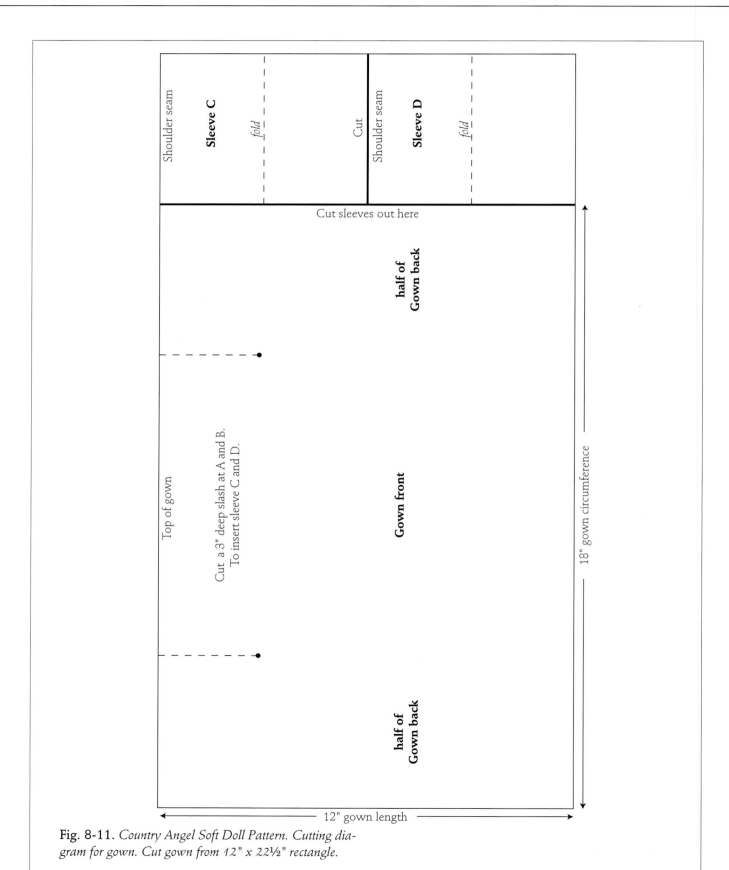

Fig. 8-11. *Country Angel Soft Doll Pattern. Cutting diagram for gown. Cut gown from 12" x 22½" rectangle.*

* ARTWORK RECIPE 31:

Decorative Hanging Mobiles

We live in a 1935 brick colonial in North-west Washington, DC. Our street has several houses that repeat. It is interesting to see the same yellow-and-black, lavender-and-black, and green-and-black bathroom tile, the same elegant, inlaid oak floors, and the same floor plan in some of the houses. During the 25 years we've lived here, a modest amount of renovation has been done on the block. But our house is much the same as it was when we brought our six-month-old firstborn here a lifetime ago. The same modest brass chande-lier hangs in the dining room and a round bas-ket lamp brought back from our honeymoon in Germany casts a pattern of weaving lights and shadows on the center hall's ceiling and walls.

From these light fixtures, mobiles made from paper hang from black quilting thread. These light-hearted decorations, like framed artwork from children, appeal to me and keep our home young at heart. Fig. 8-12, p. 180, gives patterns for some seasonal mobiles. I hang an uneven number — seven or so — per chandelier. Making them is simple and self-explanatory. Fig. 8-13, p. 181, is a mobile of doves of different sizes. My version has them cut of deep purple, hand-marbleized cotton fused to heavy art paper. Bold, silver metallic marker outlines their cut edges and glints under the lights. Interspersed hearts carry wishes for my husband to have a happy birth-day. These doves are pretty and hard to take down! They would serve as well to decorate a bridal shower, announce a newborn baby, or welcome someone home who lives away.

* ARTWORK RECIPE 32:

Birthday Banner

Family birthdays here are spontaneous and special, but casual. On the day, some of the family make cards and a simple dinner is prepared. For years I took the easy way out, taking the birthday child to the grocery store and telling him grandiosely that he could have any cake in the frozen food case. Over time the cakes got fancier! The children and I always decorated the outside door for the day and festooned the dining room wall with a handmade paper Happy Birthday banner. One year daughter Katya made a spectacular one. Each letter was drawn on half of an 8½" x 11" piece of paper and filled in with different designs in bold marker, each letter a different color. We saved it and for years simply taped a different number in for the birthday. When my niece turned 30, we faxed the whole ban-ner to her office in Chicago, announcing to her and her fellow architects, "Happy 30th Birthday!" It was attention-getting. Nonethe-less, I've dreamed of having a family Birthday Banner made of sturdier materials. Figs. 8-14A–C, p. 182–184, give all the letters needed to bond a Happy Birthday in cloth to large size file cards. From the back, hinge them together with clear, heavy packaging tape. Put reinforced tabs at the top on either end of the banner. Punch a hole in each for a ribbon to hang the banner from one window to another or simply across the wall.

Fig. 8-12. *Patterns for mobiles.*

Fig. 8-13. *Stan's Birthday Doves.*

Fig. 8-14A and 8-14B (right). *Happy Birthday Banner.*

Fig. 8-14C. *Happy Birthday Banner.*

PANSIES

Supplies
- ⅝" *wide x 10" long shaded wired ribbon*
- *4mm Heirloom Sylk® ribbon for centers*

- Fold ribbon in a U-shape (Fig. D).
- Running stitch as shown, then pull to gather into three petals.
- Stitch pansies to cloth, tucking seams beneath them. Fill the centers with French knots done in 4mm Heirloom Sylk® ribbon for embroidery (Fig. E).
- *Card note:* Glue pansies to card stock. Glue seed beads to fill their centers.

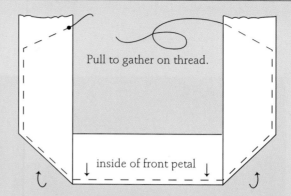

Pull to gather on thread.

inside of front petal

Fig. D.

Fig. E.

Card 8-1. *Card and fabric doll on the left made by Elly Sienkiewicz. Fabric doll on the right made by Kathleen Brassfield.*

Card 8-2. *Made by Elly Sienkiewicz.*

Card 8-3, 8-4, and 8-5. *Made by Elly Sienkiewicz.*

Card 8-7. *Made by Betty Alderman, © 1992.*

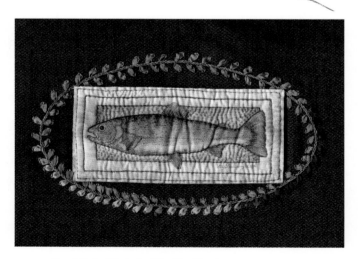

Card 8-6. *Made by Elly Sienkiewicz.*

Appliqué Paper Greetings — Elly Sienkiewicz

Part Three

The
Pattern Section

These patterns are all given full size. Whenever a template shape is cut out of fused fabric, it is cut right on the line, and no seam allowance is added. The term fuse is used throughout the book to mean fusing the plastic bonding web to the fabric. The term bond is used throughout the book to mean bonding the fused fabric to the paper.

Some of the patterns in this section are pictured throughout the book; notations are made so you can easily reference the cards. The remainder of the patterns are provided so you can create your own cards — let your imagination soar.

Enjoy this book and expand on its ideas. You may teach project classes from it or teach it lesson by lesson. You may make supply kits for projects from it and sell the kits or the finished projects or both. To protect the copyright, the author and publisher give permission to make up to two photocopies of a pattern for personal use only.

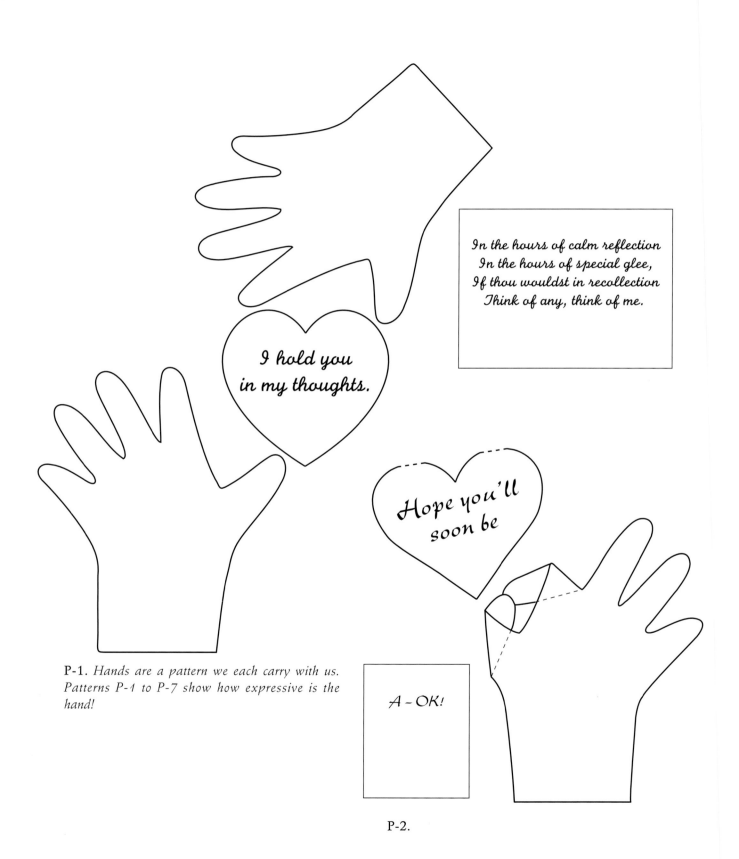

In the hours of calm reflection
In the hours of special glee,
If thou wouldst in recollection
Think of any, think of me.

I hold you
in my thoughts.

Hope you'll
soon be

P-1. *Hands are a pattern we each carry with us. Patterns P-1 to P-7 show how expressive is the hand!*

A - OK!

P-2.

Shhh...
Secrets!

P-3. *Hinged heart-cut, double on-the-fold, opens to show a message inside.*

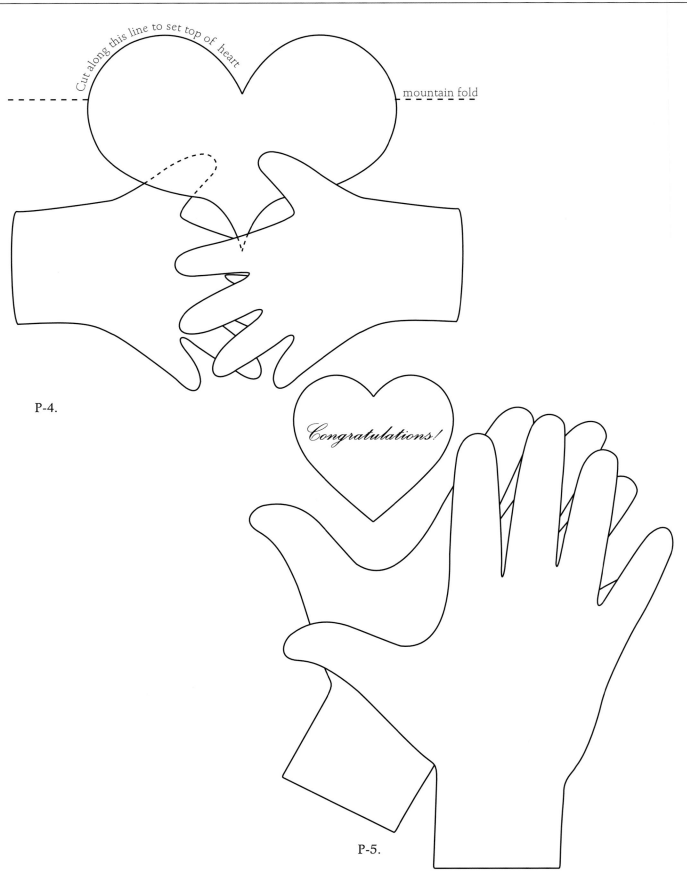

Cut along this line to set top of heart

mountain fold

P-4.

Congratulations!

P-5.

Appliqué Paper Greetings — Elly Sienkiewicz

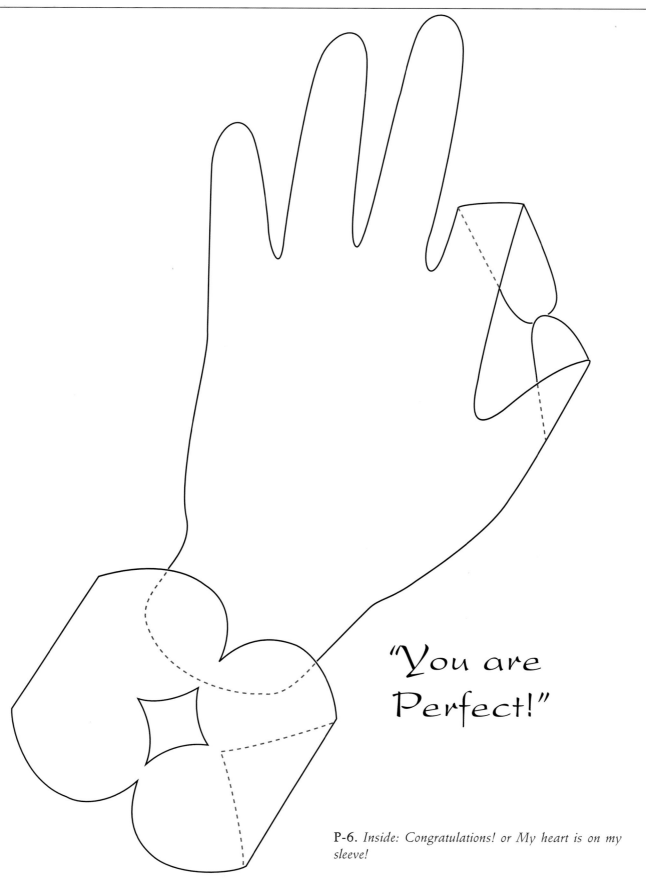

"You are Perfect!"

P-6. *Inside: Congratulations! or My heart is on my sleeve!*

P-7.

P-8.

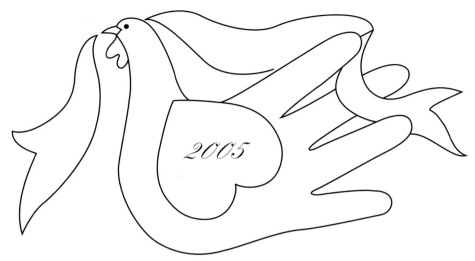

P-9. *Enlarge 200%.*

P-10. *Cut the line which forms the eyebrows and nose.*
Lift these features up for dimension. Enlarge 200%.

P-11.

P-12.

P-13.

P-14. *Shown on p. 42.*

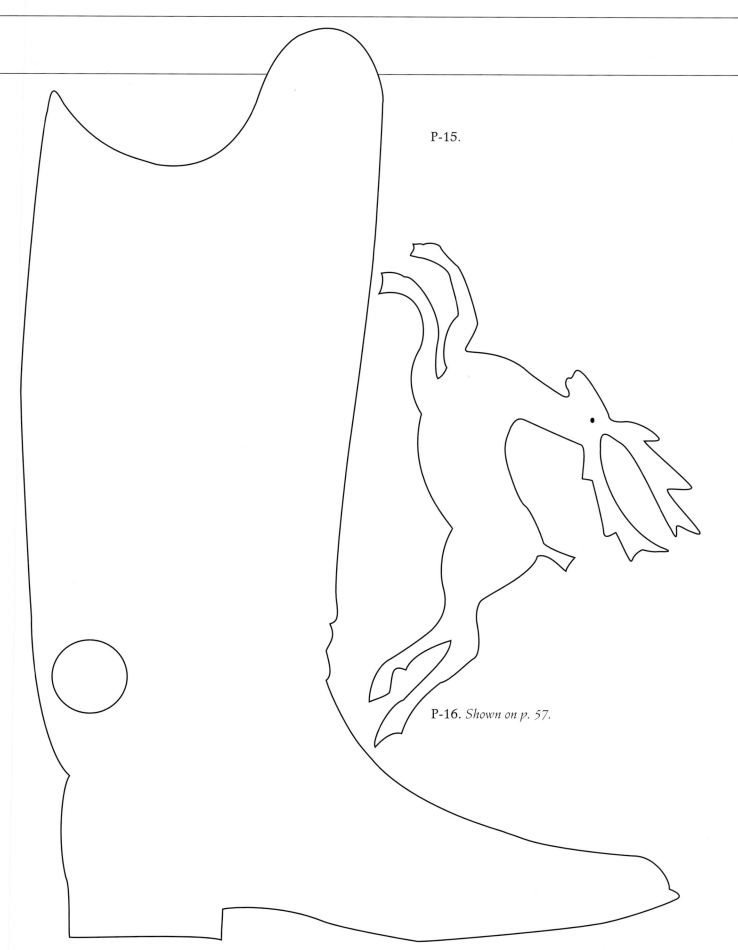

P-15.

P-16. *Shown on p. 57.*

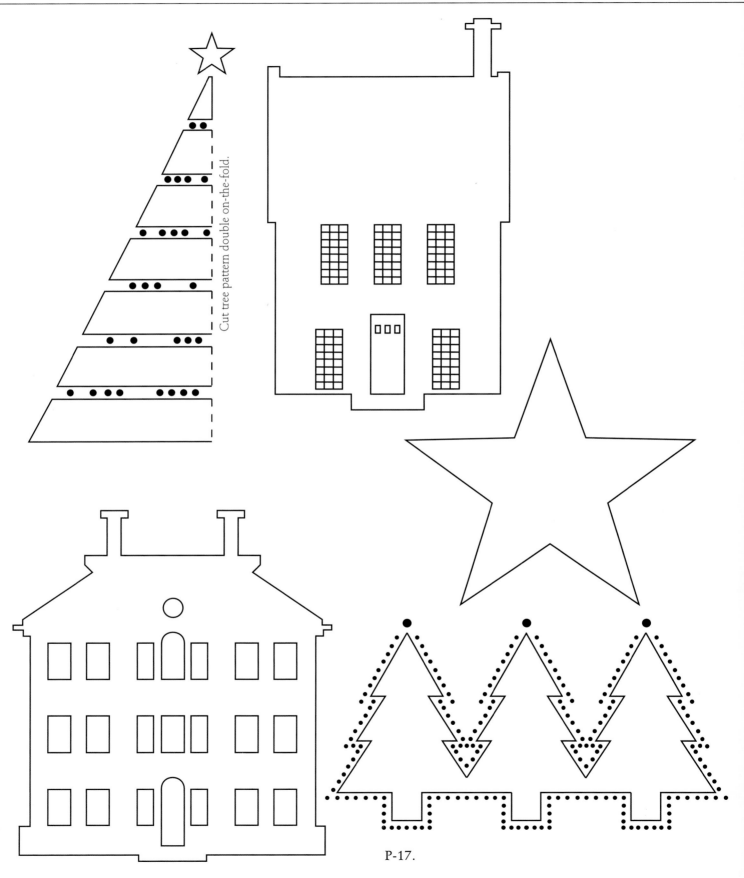

Cut tree pattern double on-the-fold.

P-17.

1999   "*And angels shall watch over thee.*"

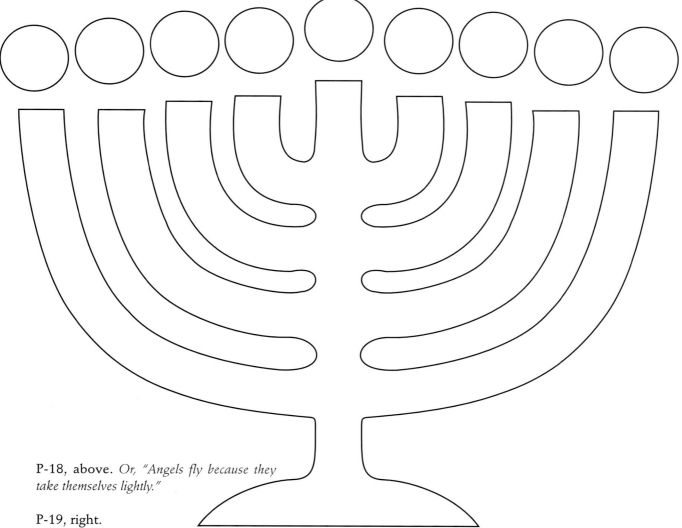

P-18, above. *Or, "Angels fly because they take themselves lightly."*

P-19, right.

mountain
fold

valley
fold

top

Cut a template out double on-the-fold.

P-20.

Above. *Enlarge 200%, card shown on p. 96.*

Above. *Shown on p. 44.*

P-21.

CONGRATULATIONS!

P-22.

Happy Birth day!

P-23.

Shown on p. 78.

P-24.

P-25. *Shown on p. 58.*

Happy 1999!

Inside:

Old trees are like old friends.
They tie us to our past;
They give stability to our present,
And they promise hope for the future.

P-26.

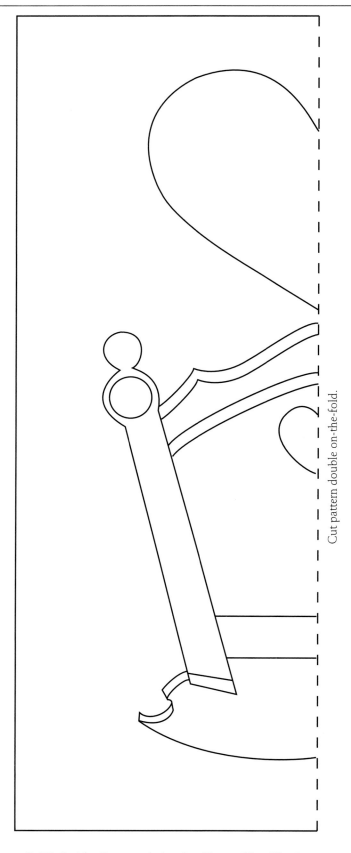

Cut pattern double on-the-fold.

P-27. *Inside: Congratulations! or Happy New Year!*

Appliqué Paper Greetings – Elly Sienkiewicz

Author's Afterword

My father was a simple man. Though he died 25 years ago, his down-to-earth wisdom stays with me, so often proven true. He combined intellectual genius with an almost saintly love for his fellow man. It seemed to me that simple, reasonable rules guided his life. He was a spiritual man and humble. Neither pettiness nor insecurity interfered with his general benevolence, though he was quick to righteous anger, and, when we children were young, he was impatient with non-compliance. He believed it was important, my mother explained, that we obey without argument in case of emergency. Even on moral issues, he relied on reason. What, he would ask of some questionable action I had proposed, if everyone did it? Like the Golden Rule, that question cut to the heart of the matter. You either accepted responsibility for making the world a better place. Or you made it worse.

From before I was born, my father had multiple sclerosis. Though my parents protected us children from the risks of the disease, I remember my father best in my late teen and early adult years. By then I knew at least by name, the battle my parents waged. And they waged it with grace, intelligence, fierce courage, and humor. For both of them, the simplest acts of daily life became challenges to be analyzed, then routinized to accomplish them most efficiently. I remember my father during his lengthy morning ablutions commenting, "The more good habits you can make routine in life, the less of your time they will take." That truth is born out. It is a homily well paired with "Never put off until tomorrow what you can do today." We each can see those who prosper from nurturing good habits and industry, and those who struggle against bad habits and procrastination.

Daddy was also a renowned physicist. Yet, growing up I learned from him the stuff of life, not of physics. He had a quiet joy in being alive. As life's simplest requirements increasingly challenged his physical abilities, he made life's daily mechanics into something of a game. For example, he had to take an astonishing number of pills. He would see how many he could consume in one swallow. I came to love the smile of accomplishment which capped a one-swallow start to the day! He arose from bed and got into a wheelchair only with my mother's help. "One, two, three...swing!" he would chant, so that the little woman and the big man pivoted in unison. He never failed to thank her and show his appreciation. All his habits that I remember are good ones!

In my middle years now, I look back on a substantial length of life lived and commend some habits, while working to change others. Some thrifty habits that had served my husband and me well when we were young and poor, fell into disuse when time became as precious as money. (Or when working for money left so little time and energy!) These days a happier equilibrium is being reached. "Moderation in all things" is the ancient Greek ideal whose truth seems perpetually rediscovered. After a lifetime of increasing mechanization, so many these days seek joy in doing a task the old way — baking a cake from scratch, walking to run an errand, or picnicking on a road trip rather than stopping for fast food.

For decades my home town has been Washington, DC, our nation's capital. Even here, I've noticed much of the city's citizens slowing to savor life's simpler pleasures. Every year more annual flowers are planted to bloom in her characteristic small city gardens. Sipping coffee in cafés and savoring fresh bread from neighborhood bakeries are currently the rage, while summers still bring the tempting smells and friendly visits over backyard barbecues. Even the record-breaking snows of this past winter brought my street nightly neighborhood pot-luck suppers for several days, as though the harsh temperatures gave community a higher valuation in our daily scheme of things. How rich these simple pleasures, these habits by which we steer our life and confirm how good it is to be alive.

Some good habits are as natural to us as our disposition. As my father observed so long ago, they guide us effortlessly and liberate us. But initiating new good habits takes effort. We must free a time and place for an incipient good habit, substituting the better for the less rewarding. The making of paper greetings can itself be a useful exercise in forming positive habits! Do you want to confine life's necessary but less fulfilling tasks to a smaller portion of your time? Would you like to reduce routine expenditures and the frenetic pace of shopping for every little thing? Do you long to make your token presents, thereby visiting a bit with the person whom you will gift? Do you aspire to let someone know that they are special and that you care?

If the answer to any of these questions is yes, then you'll find making paper greetings a delightful process. They are relatively inexpensive and quick, especially when the sup-

plies are corralled, and the workplace organized. Their making becomes one more good habit! For me, the struggle is continuous, of trying to routinize life's good habits, to husband my time and money, to nurture connections with friends and family, and to savor the moment. My recent habit of making paper greetings has seemed a good one that may stick. As you've noted in this book, paper greetings include the making of cards as well as the construction and packaging of small, mailable gifts. They cost less in time and money, are more fun for me than shopping, and are more appreciated by the recipient than a store-bought card, telephone-ordered flowers, or what luck and lots of looking can find in an affordable memento. I hope creating paper greetings may suit your needs as well. That it will provide you great pleasure, I have no doubt!

Elly Sienkiewicz
Washington, DC
January 6, 1997

Other AQS Books

This is only a small selection of the books available from the American Quilter's Society. AQS books are known worldwide for timely topics, clear writing, beautiful color photos, and accurate illustrations and patterns. The following books are available from your local bookseller, quilt shop, or public library.

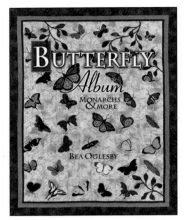

#6674   us$19.95

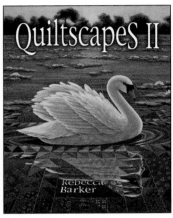

#6680   us$21.95

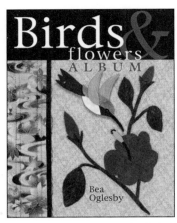

#6211   us$19.95

#6300   us$24.95

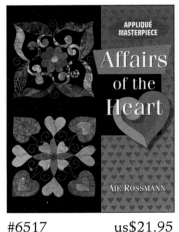

#6517   us$21.95

#6077   us$24.95

#6511   us$22.95

#6295   us$24.95

#5588   us$24.95

Look for these books nationally.
Call or **Visit** our Web site at

1-800-626-5420
www.AmericanQuilter.com